Sweet dress book

23 STYLISH OUTFITS FROM
SIX SIMPLE PATTERNS

Yoshiko Tsukiori

Laurence King Publishing

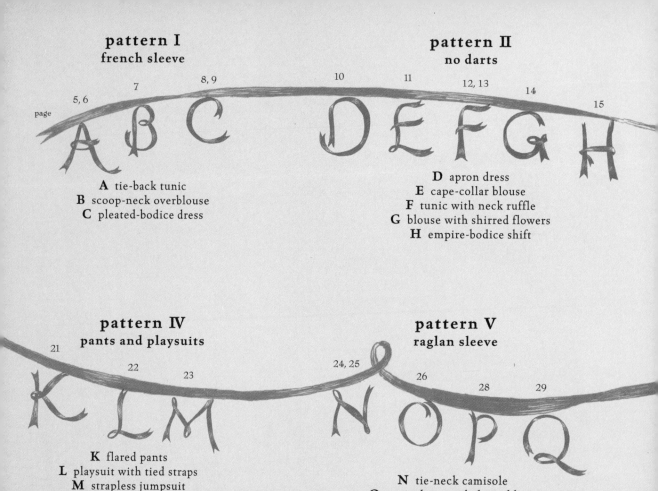

pattern I
french sleeve

page 5, 6 7 8, 9

A B C

A tie-back tunic
B scoop-neck overblouse
C pleated-bodice dress

pattern II
no darts

10 11 12, 13 14 15

D E F G H

D apron dress
E cape-collar blouse
F tunic with neck ruffle
G blouse with shirred flowers
H empire-bodice shift

pattern IV
pants and playsuits

21 22 23

K L M

K flared pants
L playsuit with tied straps
M strapless jumpsuit

pattern V
raglan sleeve

24, 25 26 28 29

N O P Q

N tie-neck camisole
O tunic dress with draped hem
P ruffle-trim coat dress
Q tucked-bodice blouse

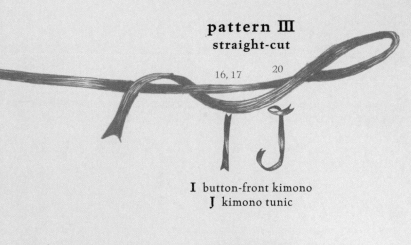

pattern III
straight-cut

16, 17   20

I button-front kimono
J kimono tunic

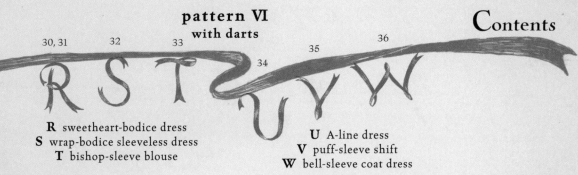

pattern VI
with darts

Contents

0, 31   32   33   35   36
                                    34

R sweetheart-bodice dress
S wrap-bodice sleeveless dress
T bishop-sleeve blouse

U A-line dress
V puff-sleeve shift
W bell-sleeve coat dress

Including the basic patterns and their variations, I have produced a total of 23 garment designs to suit the adult woman, dividing them into six categories:

"french sleeve," "no darts," "straight-cut," "pants and playsuits," "raglan sleeve," and "with darts."

These clothes combine adult sophistication with some cute touches, without being too indulgent.

I hope you enjoy making them.

Yoshiko Tsukiori

A

pattern I
french sleeve

sewing instructions p. 42

tie-back tunic

pattern I features french-sleeve designs for a tunic, overblouse, and dress

β **pattern I**
french sleeve
sewing instructions p. 44

scoop-neck overblouse

pattern I
french sleeve

sewing instructions p. 46

pleated-bodice dress

 pattern **II**
no darts

sewing instructions p. 48

apron dress

pattern II
no darts

sewing instructions p. 50

cape-collar blouse

pattern II features designs without bodice darts for an apron dress, blouses, tunic, and shift dress

F pattern **II**
no darts

sewing instructions p. 52

tunic with neck ruffle

G pattern II
no darts

sewing instructions p. 54

blouse with shirred flowers

H pattern II
no darts
sewing instructions p. 56

empire-bodice shift

pattern III
straight-cut

sewing instructions p. 58

button-front kimono

pattern III features two straight-cut kimono designs for you to make

Cupcakes

Ingredients

¹/₃ cup (75 g) butter
²/₃ cup (85 g) brown sugar
1 egg
1 cup (135 g) flour
¹/₈ cup (15 g) ground almonds
¹/₂ tbsp (7 ml) baking powder
5 tbsp (70 ml) milk

Icing, dragees, sugar decorations, etc.—quantity to suit

Allow the egg, butter, and milk to return to room temperature
Sift the flour, ground almonds, and baking powder together (*a)

Preheat the oven to 350°F / 180°C / Gas mark 4

Recipe

1 Whip the butter with an electric mixer and add the brown
   sugar in two or three batches, combining thoroughly each
   time until the mixture is pale and fluffy.

2 Beat the egg and add it to the mixture in five or six batches.
   The mixture will separate if the egg is too cold, so first leave
   the egg in warm water of about 95°F (35°C), or warm it
   gently on the stove without allowing it to cook.

3 Add about one third of the flour mixture (*a) and combine
   using a rubber spatula, folding the mixture up from the
   bottom of the bowl. While the mixture is still floury, add
   one third of the milk and mix rapidly, repeating this step
   twice more until all of the flour and milk have been added.

4 Put the baking cups in the muffin pan and spoon the mixture
   into the cups almost to the top.

5 Place in the preheated oven and bake for around 20 minutes.
   When the cakes appear done, leave them to cool on a cooling rack.

6 Decorate with your favorite icing and dragees or sugar decorations.

pattern III
straight-cut

sewing instructions p. 60

kimono tunic

pattern IV features pant designs, including flared pants, a playsuit, and a strapless jumpsuit

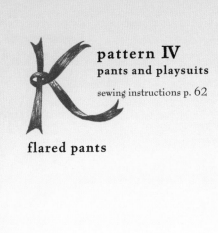

pattern IV
pants and playsuits
sewing instructions p. 62

flared pants

 pattern **IV**
pants and playsuits

sewing instructions p. 64

playsuit with tied straps

pattern **IV**
pants and playsuits
sewing instructions p. 66

strapless jumpsuit

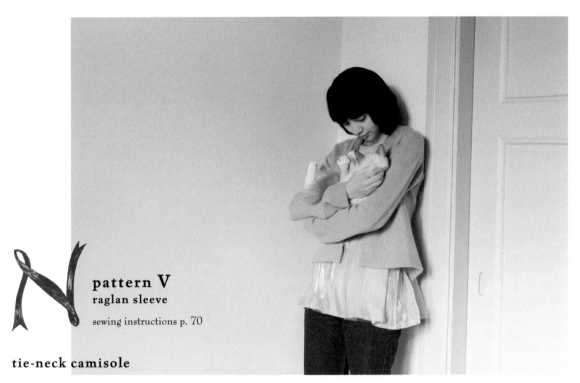

N **pattern V**
raglan sleeve

sewing instructions p. 70

tie-neck camisole

pattern V features raglan-sleeve designs for a camisole, tunic dress, coat dress, and blouse

pattern V
raglan sleeve

sewing instructions p. 72

tunic dress with draped hem

pattern V
raglan sleeve

sewing instructions p. 74

ruffle-trim coat dress

Q pattern **V**
raglan sleeve

sewing instructions p. 76

tucked-bodice blouse

 pattern **VI**
with darts

sewing instructions p. 78

sweetheart-bodice dress

pattern VI features designs with bodice darts for a shift, dresses, a blouse, and a coat dress

S pattern VI
with darts

sewing instructions p. 80

wrap-bodice sleeveless dress

pattern VI
with darts
sewing instructions p. 82

bishop-sleeve blouse

pattern **VI**
with darts

sewing instructions p. 84

A-line dress

pattern VI
with darts

sewing instructions p. 67

puff-sleeve shift

pattern **VI**
with darts

sewing instructions p. 86

bell-sleeve coat dress

Sewing instructions

Dressmaking basics

I have summarized the basic techniques you will need to make the designs in this book in the **Basics** section on pp. 38–41, which covers the following:

- Marking up a pattern piece
- Threefold and double-fold hems
- Making bias binding from the same fabric as your garment
- Using bias binding … to add piping
- Using bias binding … to create a facing-like finish

About the sizes used in this book

- The designs in this book can be made in four sizes: XS, S, M, and L.
- Choose the pattern piece that matches your size by referring to the table of measurements below.
- The heights are the same for each size, so you can adjust the length to suit your preference.
- Sets of four numbers that appear in some of the instructions or drawings represent the measurements for sizes XS, S, M, and L, in that order.

Fabrics and cutting techniques

- In the instructions in this book, fabrics that have only one measurement share the same length for sizes XS through L.
- The layout that you choose for cutting the fabric may be different depending on the size you are making, so it is a good idea to lay all of the pattern pieces out first so that you can check them before you make any cuts.
- The length of the bias binding (which will usually be in the same fabric as you use for the main part of the design) will be different for each size.
- Refer to the widths and cutting positions shown in the cutting layouts and take measurements for the neckline, armholes, and other sections of the design that you are working on in order to be sure of obtaining the right length.
- Unless stipulated otherwise, the seam allowance is ⅜ in (1 cm).

Table of reference measurements   Units: in (cm)

	XS	S	M	L
Bust	30¾ (78)	32⅝ (83)	34⅝ (88)	36⅝ (93)
Waist	23¼ (59)	25¼ (64)	27⅛ (69)	29⅛ (74)
Hips	33⅞ (86)	35⅜ (90)	37 (94)	38⅝ (98)
Height	63 (160)	63 (160)	63 (160)	63 (160)

Basics
Basic techniques for sewing clothes

Marking up a pattern piece

* Line up the markings for the center lines, shoulder lines, sleeve caps, and so forth at the front and back of your pattern piece and pin them with marking pins, and then stitch ⅜ in (1 cm, or the specified distance) to the inside, working to the guidelines on the throat plate of your sewing machine.

• When you have traced the full-scale pattern piece, add a seam allowance (of ⅜ in/ 1 cm unless specified otherwise), and then cut the fabric.

• Mark each point by notching or using a needle punch (awl).

• Mark the center front and opening ends (these markings will help guide you when you align the facings).

1 Cut off a diagonal corner of approx. ⅛ in (0.3 cm) at the center front of the neckline.

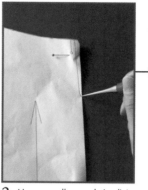

2 Use a needle punch (awl) to make a hole at the edge on the opening end.

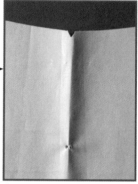

3 The hole will look like this.

• Mark the bodice dart.

1 Make a notch of around ⅛ in (0.3 cm) in the lines forming the top and bottom of the bodice dart.

2 Use a needle punch (awl) to make a hole at the tip of the bodice dart.

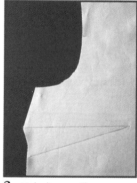

3 Make lines on the wrong side to connect the notches with the hole.

• Mark the shoulder lines and sleeves (this will guide you as to the width of the seam allowance when you sew the shoulders).

1 Make a notch of approx. ⅛ in (0.3 cm) in the shoulder line on the neckline side.

2 Make notches of approx. ⅛ in (0.3 cm) at the sleeve markings or gather ends.

3 The marked pattern piece.

Threefold and double-fold hems

• Threefold (for a ¾ in/2 cm-wide hem)

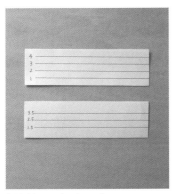

* Making an ironing ruler
Mark a piece of card (about postcard thickness, approx. 7 in x 2 in/20 cm x 5 cm) with parallel lines drawn ⅜ in (1 cm) apart.

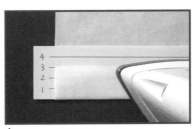

1 Make a 1⅛ in (3 cm) fold using an ironing ruler.

2 Staying in this position, fold in to the ¾ in (2 cm) line of the ironing ruler.

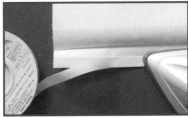

3 Attach double-sided fusible stay tape to the folded-in seam allowance instead of basting (or, alternatively, pin with marking pins).

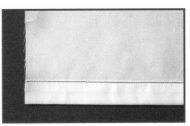

4 Stitch in a line ¹⁄₃₂ in to ¹⁄₁₆ in (0.1 cm to 0.2 cm) from the edge.

• Narrow threefold (for a ⅜ in/1 cm-wide hem).

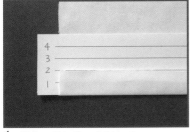

1 Make a ¾ in (2 cm) fold using an ironing ruler.

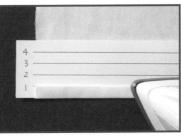

2 Staying in this position, fold in to the ¾ in (2 cm) line of the ironing ruler.

3 Stitch in a line ¹⁄₃₂ in to ¹⁄₁₆ in (0.1 cm to 0.2 cm) from the edge.

• Double-fold hem

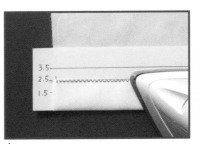

1 Overlock or zigzag the edge of the fabric. For a 1 in (2.5 cm) seam allowance, fold to a width of 1 in (2.5 cm) using an ironing ruler.

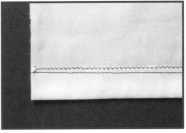

2 Stitch in a line approx. ³⁄₁₆ in (0.5 cm) from the edge.

Basics

Making bias binding from the same fabric as your garment

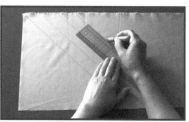

1 Draw a straight bias line at 45 degrees to the grain (following the indications on the relevant cutting layout for positioning and width). Use a clear ruler to draw parallel lines, and cut.

2 Feed the bias binding through the bias binding maker.

3 Pull the fabric through gradually, and it will come out with both sides folded.

4 Press the folded fabric.

* Joining the strips together

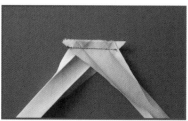

1 Fold out the creases on the bias binding and align them wrong sides out, stitching in a line ³⁄₁₆ in (0.5 cm) from the end.

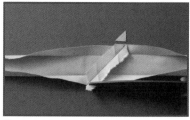

2 Press open the seam allowance and trim off the excess.

Using bias binding ...
to add piping

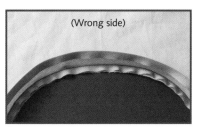

(Wrong side)

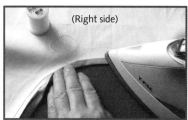

(Right side)

1 Working from the wrong side of the fabric, sew along the curve (of the neckline and armholes) in line with the crease (there will be ease on the inside of the curve, which will stand up on the outside).

2 Turn onto the right side, lay the bias binding over the seam in step 1, and press. At this stage, any fusible threads in the fabric will melt with the heat from the iron, which provides a handy substitute for basting (if this does not work, pin with marking pins).

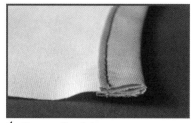

3 Stitch in a line ½₂ in (0.1 cm) from the edge.

4 Cross-sectional view.

Using bias binding ...
to create a facing-like finish

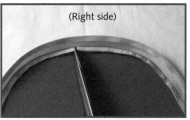

(Right side)

(Wrong side)

1 Working from the right side of the fabric, align the edge of the binding (for the neckline and armholes) with the curve, and sew along the crease (there will be ease on the inside of the curve). Add notches as deep as the seam in the seam allowance of the curve (being careful not to cut into the seam itself).

2 Turn onto the wrong side, fold the seam line, and iron the edge. Stretch the edge out to shape into the bodice. At this stage, any fusible threads in the fabric will melt with the heat from the iron, which provides a handy substitute for basting (if this does not work, pin with marking pins).

(Wrong side)

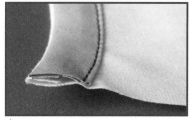

3 Stitch in a line ½₂ in (0.1 cm) from the edge.

4 Cross-sectional view.

page
5

pattern I
french sleeve

tie-back tunic

Fabric

Fabric [cotton print]: W 43¼ in x L 74¾ in (110 cm x 190 cm).

*If your fabric has a one-way print, be sure the pattern pieces are aligned in the same direction.

Instructions

Preparation: Overlock or zigzag the seam allowance on the sides of the bodices.

1 Sew the tucks in the front bodice (turning them toward the center).
2 Sew the shoulders (overlock or zigzag the seam allowance on both pieces at the same time. Turn the seam allowance toward the back).
3 Sew the sides (press open the side seam allowance).
4 Sew the cuffs with a threefold hem (see p. 39).
5 Make a threefold hem.
6 Make the drawstrings.
7 Sew the center back with a threefold hem, sandwiching the drawstrings.
8 Pipe the neckline with the bias binding (in the same fabric as the bodice (see pp. 40–41) and sew the drawstrings at the same time.

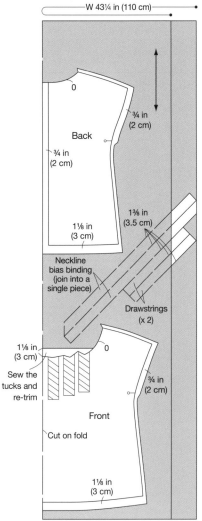

Cutting layout

W 43¼ in (110 cm)

0

Back

¾ in (2 cm)

¾ in (2 cm)

1⅜ in (3.5 cm)

1⅛ in (3 cm)

Neckline bias binding (join into a single piece)

Drawstrings (x 2)

1⅛ in (3 cm)

Sew the tucks and re-trim

0

¾ in (2 cm)

Front

Cut on fold

1⅛ in (3 cm)

1

2

5

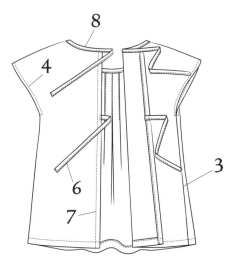

8

4

3

6

7

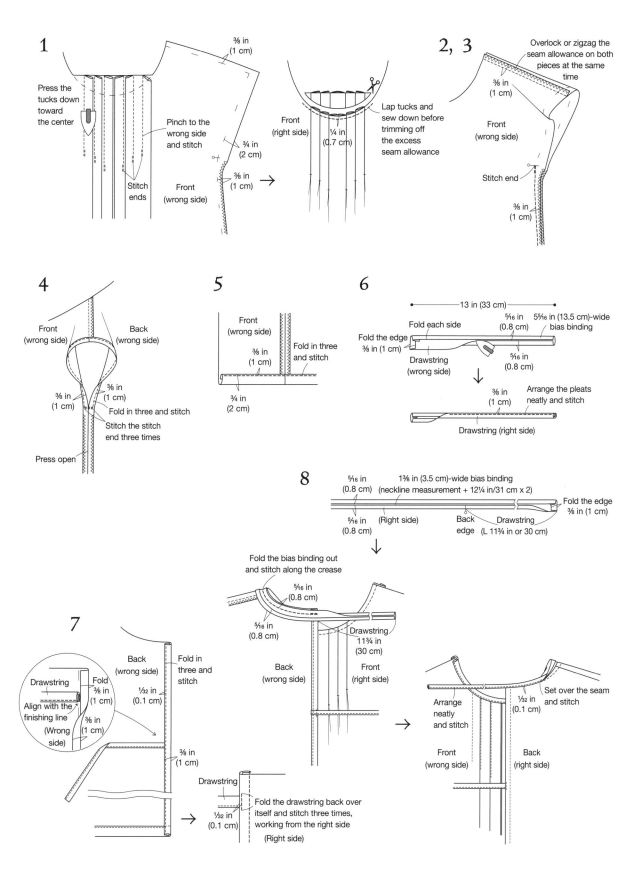

1

Press the tucks down toward the center

Pinch to the wrong side and stitch

Stitch ends

Front (wrong side)

⅜ in (1 cm)

¾ in (2 cm)

⅜ in (1 cm)

Front (right side)

¼ in (0.7 cm)

Lap tucks and sew down before trimming off the excess seam allowance

2, 3

Overlock or zigzag the seam allowance on both pieces at the same time

⅜ in (1 cm)

Front (wrong side)

Stitch end

⅜ in (1 cm)

4

Front (wrong side)

Back (wrong side)

⅜ in (1 cm)

⅜ in (1 cm)

Fold in three and stitch

Stitch the stitch end three times

Press open

5

Front (wrong side)

⅜ in (1 cm)

Fold in three and stitch

¾ in (2 cm)

6

13 in (33 cm)

Fold each side

Fold the edge ⅜ in (1 cm)

Drawstring (wrong side)

5⁄16 in (0.8 cm)

5⁄16 in (0.8 cm)

5⁵⁄16 in (13.5 cm)-wide bias binding

⅜ in (1 cm)

Arrange the pleats neatly and stitch

Drawstring (right side)

8

5⁄16 in (0.8 cm)

1⅜ in (3.5 cm)-wide bias binding (neckline measurement + 12¼ in/31 cm x 2)

5⁄16 in (0.8 cm)

(Right side)

Back edge

Drawstring (L 11¾ in or 30 cm)

Fold the edge ⅜ in (1 cm)

Fold the bias binding out and stitch along the crease

5⁄16 in (0.8 cm)

5⁄16 in (0.8 cm)

Back (wrong side)

Front (right side)

Drawstring 11¾ in (30 cm)

Arrange neatly and stitch

Set over the seam and stitch

1⁄32 in (0.1 cm)

Front (wrong side)

Back (right side)

7

Drawstring

Align with the finishing line (Wrong side)

Fold ⅜ in (1 cm)

⅜ in (1 cm)

Back (wrong side)

Fold in three and stitch

1⁄32 in (0.1 cm)

⅜ in (1 cm)

Drawstring

1⁄32 in (0.1 cm)

Fold the drawstring back over itself and stitch three times, working from the right side

(Right side)

pattern I
french sleeve

scoop-neck overblouse

Fabric

Fabric [double cotton gauze]: W 44⅞ in x L 102⅜ in (114 cm x 260 cm)

Instructions

Preparation: Overlock or zigzag the seam allowance around the collar ruffles and sleeve ruffles.

1 Sew the collar ruffles and sleeve ruffles with a double-fold hem (see p. 39) (except at the ends you are attaching to the bodice), and then make a gathering stitch in two rows on the edge that is going to be attached.

2 Sew the shoulders (overlock or zigzag the seam allowance on both pieces at the same time. Turn the seam allowance toward the back).

3 Attach the collar ruffle to the bodice (see p. 45 steps 1 to 3). (Overlock or zigzag the seam allowance of the armholes on both layers of fabric and the sides at the same time as far as the hem. Turn the seam allowance toward the bodice.)

4 Attach the collar ruffles to the bodice in the same way as the sleeve ruffles (see p. 45 steps 1 to 3), and then gather the front and back necklines.

5 Pipe the neckline with the bias binding (using the same fabric as for the bodice) (see pp. 40–41).

6 Sew the sides (press open the side seam allowance) and backstitch the bottom of the sleeve opening.

7 Stitch the armholes.

8 Make a threefold hem (see p. 39).

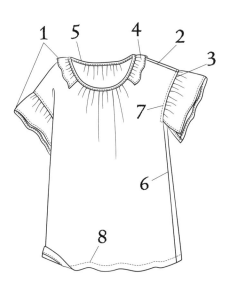

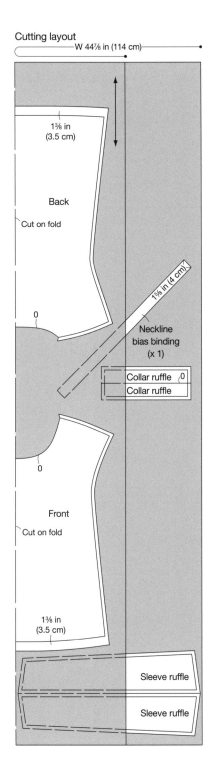

Cutting layout

W 44⅞ in (114 cm)

1⅜ in (3.5 cm)

Back

Cut on fold

0

1⅝ in (4 cm)

Neckline bias binding (x 1)

Collar ruffle   0
Collar ruffle

0

Front

Cut on fold

1⅜ in (3.5 cm)

Sleeve ruffle

Sleeve ruffle

Adding gathers and attaching the ruffles

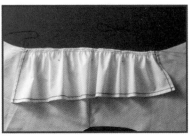

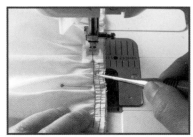

1 Stitch around the edge of the sleeve ruffle with a double-fold hem. Sew two rows of large gathering stitches ¹⁄₁₆ in (0.2 cm) and ⁵⁄₁₆ in (0.8 cm) from the edge of the ruffle that you are attaching to the bodice. Align the bodice and sleeve ruffles wrong sides out, then align the ruffle ends and shoulder lines of the front and back armholes and pin with marking pins.

2 Pull the threads of the gathering stitches to create the gathers.

3 Stitch with your sewing machine, working with a needle punch (awl) to keep the fabric neat and ensure that the gathers are even.

4 Overlock or zigzag the seam allowances on both layers at the same time, fold toward the bodice and then, working from the right side, stitch in a line ⁵⁄₁₆ in (0.8 cm) from the edge.

5 As seen from the wrong side.

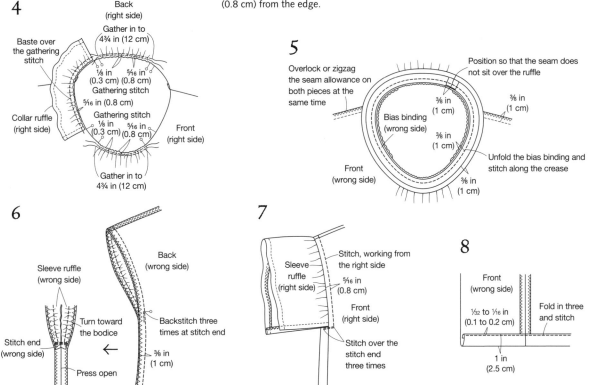

4
- Back (right side)
- Gather in to 4¾ in (12 cm)
- Baste over the gathering stitch
- ⅛ in (0.3 cm) ⁵⁄₁₆ in (0.8 cm)
- Gathering stitch ⁵⁄₁₆ in (0.8 cm)
- Collar ruffle (right side)
- Gathering stitch ⅛ in (0.3 cm) ⁵⁄₁₆ in (0.8 cm)
- Front (right side)
- Gather in to 4¾ in (12 cm)

5
- Overlock or zigzag the seam allowance on both pieces at the same time
- Position so that the seam does not sit over the ruffle
- ⅜ in (1 cm)
- ⅜ in (1 cm)
- Bias binding (wrong side)
- ⅜ in (1 cm)
- Front (wrong side)
- Unfold the bias binding and stitch along the crease
- ⅜ in (1 cm)

6
- Sleeve ruffle (wrong side)
- Back (wrong side)
- Turn toward the bodice
- Backstitch three times at stitch end
- Stitch end (wrong side)
- Press open
- ⅜ in (1 cm)

7
- Sleeve ruffle (right side)
- Stitch, working from the right side ⁵⁄₁₆ in (0.8 cm)
- Front (right side)
- Stitch over the stitch end three times

8
- Front (wrong side)
- ¹⁄₃₂ to ¹⁄₁₆ in (0.1 to 0.2 cm)
- Fold in three and stitch
- 1 in (2.5 cm)

pattern I
french sleeve

pleated-bodice dress

Fabric

Fabric [cotton and linen print]: W 43¼ in x L 86⅝ in
   (110 cm x 220 cm)

*If your fabric has a large, one-way print repeat and
   you want to match it up, be sure to buy at least
   20 in (50 cm) extra.

*If your fabric has a one-way print, be sure the
   pattern pieces are aligned in the same direction.

Fusible interfacing (for the neckline facing):
   W 35⅜ in x L 7⅞ in (90 cm x L 20 cm)

Button: ⅝ in (1.5 cm) diameter x 1

Instructions

Preparation: Attach the fusible interfacing to the
   front neckline facing and back neckline facing.
   (See "How to sew the facing," p. 47.)

1 Overlock or zigzag the seam allowance on
   the bodice sides, center back, and around the
   pockets.

2 Make and attach the pockets. Sew the tucks in
   the front bodice, turning them toward the center
   (see p. 43).

3 Sew the shoulders (overlock or zigzag the seam
   allowance on both pieces at the same time. Turn
   the seam allowance toward the back).

4 Sew the sides (press open the side seam
   allowance).

5 Sew the cuffs with a threefold hem (see pp. 39
   and 43).

6 Make the fabric loop (see p. 55).

7 Sew the center back, leaving an opening (press
   open the seam allowance).

8 Sew the shoulders of the facing (press open the
   seam allowance), and then overlock or zigzag
   the seam allowance on the innermost edge of
   the facing. Attach the fabric loop to the opening,
   align the bodice and facing wrong sides out, and
   edge-stitch the neckline.

9 Finish the opening.

10 Make a threefold hem.

11 Attach the button.

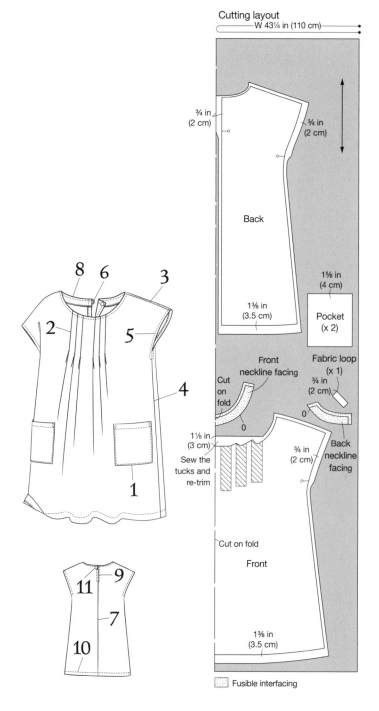

1

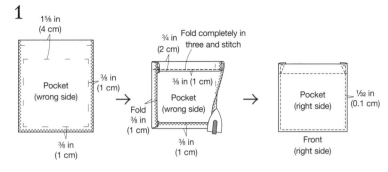

1⅝ in (4 cm)

Pocket (wrong side)

⅜ in (1 cm)

⅜ in (1 cm)

→

¾ in (2 cm)

Fold completely in three and stitch

⅜ in (1 cm)

Pocket (wrong side)

Fold ⅜ in (1 cm)

⅜ in (1 cm)

→

Pocket (right side)

¹⁄₃₂ in (0.1 cm)

Front (right side)

2

Lap the tucks over each other and sew down, and then trim off the excess seam allowance

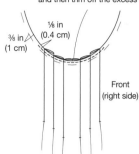

⅛ in (0.4 cm)

⅜ in (1 cm)

Front (right side)

7, 8

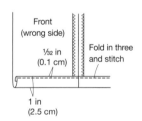

2 in (5 cm)-long fabric loop

Right back (wrong side)

¾ in (2 cm)

Opening end

Left back (wrong side)

⅜ in (1 cm)

Baste

Set over by ⅜ in (1 cm)

(Right side)

→

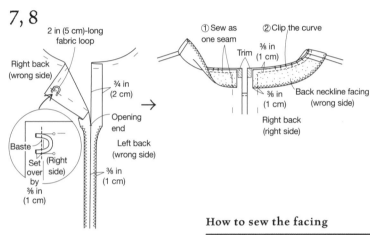

① Sew as one seam

② Clip the curve

Trim

⅜ in (1 cm)

⅜ in (1 cm)

Back neckline facing (wrong side)

Right back (right side)

9

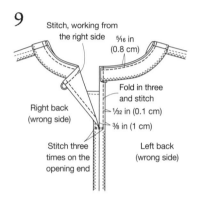

Stitch, working from the right side

⁵⁄₁₆ in (0.8 cm)

Right back (wrong side)

Fold in three and stitch

¹⁄₃₂ in (0.1 cm)

⅜ in (1 cm)

Stitch three times on the opening end

Left back (wrong side)

10

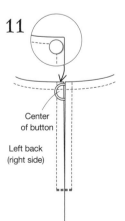

Front (wrong side)

¹⁄₃₂ in (0.1 cm)

Fold in three and stitch

1 in (2.5 cm)

11

Center of button

Left back (right side)

How to sew the facing

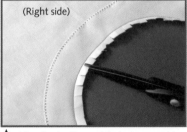

(Right side)

A Align the bodice and facing wrong sides out, align the center front and shoulder lines, pin with marking pins, and then sew. Notch the seam allowance at ⅜ in (1 cm) intervals (being careful not to cut into the seam itself).

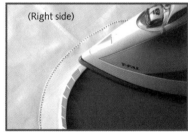

(Right side)

B With an iron, fold the seam allowance along the seam toward the facing.

(Wrong side)

(Right side)

C Turn the facing onto the right side and press neatly in place.

D Cross-sectional view.

pattern II
no darts

apron dress

Fabric

Fabric [linen]: W 55⅛ in x L 70⅞ in (140 cm x 180 cm)
Fabric [cotton stripe]: W 43¼ in x L3⅞ in (110 cm x 10 cm)
Elastic: W⅝ in x L 28⅝, 30⅝, 32⅝, or 34⅝ in (1.5 cm x 73, 78, 83, or 88 cm) (including the seam allowance)

Instructions

Preparation: Overlock or zigzag the seam allowance around the pockets.

1 Make and attach the pockets.
2 Sew the sides, leaving an opening on the left for the elastic to pass through (overlock or zigzag the seam allowance on both pieces at the same time. Turn the seam allowance toward the back).
3 Sew the top edge of the bodice with a threefold hem (see p. 39).
4 Make a threefold hem.
5 Sew the edges of the ruffles with a threefold hem (except at the edge that you are attaching to the bodice).
6 Make the front and back shoulder straps, sandwiching the ruffles in the front shoulder straps.
7 Attach the shoulder straps to the bodice. Pass the elastic through the opening.

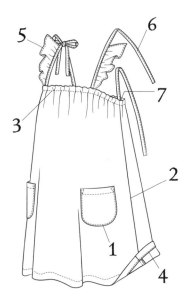

Cutting layout [linen]

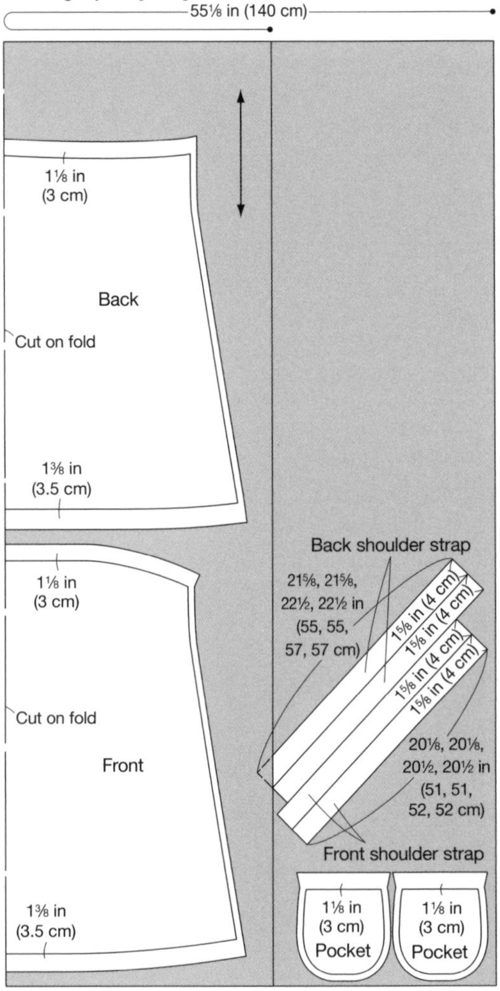

55⅛ in (140 cm)

1⅛ in (3 cm)

Back

Cut on fold

1⅜ in (3.5 cm)

1⅛ in (3 cm)

Cut on fold

Front

1⅜ in (3.5 cm)

Back shoulder strap

21⅝, 21⅝, 22½, 22½ in (55, 55, 57, 57 cm)

1⅝ in (4 cm)
1⅝ in (4 cm)
1⅝ in (4 cm)
1⅝ in (4 cm)

20⅛, 20⅛, 20½, 20½ in (51, 51, 52, 52 cm)

Front shoulder strap

1⅛ in (3 cm) Pocket

1⅛ in (3 cm) Pocket

Cutting layout [cotton stripe]

W 43¼ in (110 cm)

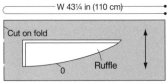

Cut on fold

0   Ruffle

1

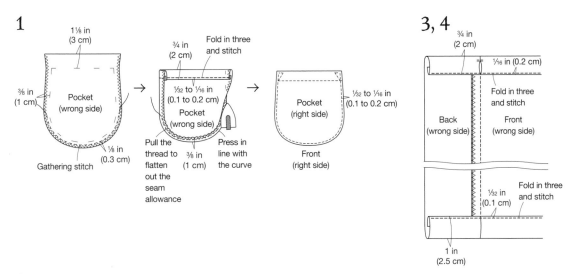

1⅛ in (3 cm)

¾ in (2 cm)

Fold in three and stitch

⅜ in (1 cm)

Pocket (wrong side)

1/32 to 1/16 in (0.1 to 0.2 cm)

Pocket (wrong side)

1/32 to 1/16 in (0.1 to 0.2 cm)

⅛ in (0.3 cm)

Gathering stitch

Pull the thread to flatten out the seam allowance

⅜ in (1 cm)

Press in line with the curve

Pocket (right side)

Front (right side)

3, 4

¾ in (2 cm)

1/16 in (0.2 cm)

Fold in three and stitch

Back (wrong side)

Front (wrong side)

1/32 in (0.1 cm)

Fold in three and stitch

1 in (2.5 cm)

2

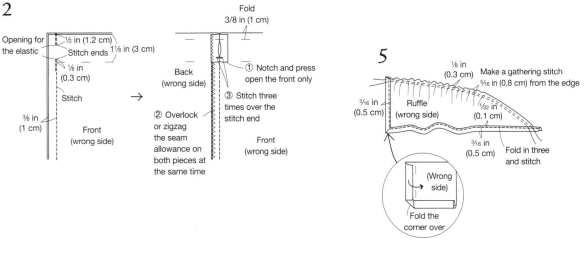

Opening for the elastic

½ in (1.2 cm)

Stitch ends

1⅛ in (3 cm)

⅛ in (0.3 cm)

Stitch

⅜ in (1 cm)

Front (wrong side)

Fold 3/8 (1 cm)

Back (wrong side)

① Notch and press open the front only

③ Stitch three times over the stitch end

② Overlock or zigzag the seam allowance on both pieces at the same time

Front (wrong side)

5

⅛ in (0.3 cm)

Make a gathering stitch 5/16 in (0.8 cm) from the edge

3/16 in (0.5 cm)

Ruffle (wrong side)

1/32 in (0.1 cm)

3/16 in (0.5 cm)

Fold in three and stitch

(Wrong side)

Fold the corner over

6

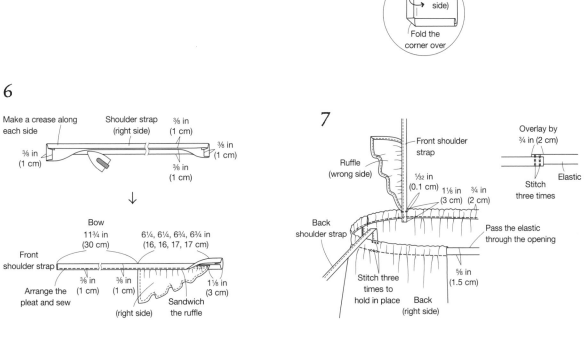

Make a crease along each side

Shoulder strap (right side)

⅜ in (1 cm)

⅜ in (1 cm)

⅜ in (1 cm)

⅜ in (1 cm)

Bow 11¾ in (30 cm)

6¼, 6¼, 6¾, 6¾ in (16, 16, 17, 17 cm)

Front shoulder strap

⅜ in (1 cm)

⅜ in (1 cm)

1⅛ in (3 cm)

Arrange the pleat and sew

(right side)

Sandwich the ruffle

7

Front shoulder strap

Ruffle (wrong side)

1/32 in (0.1 cm)

1⅛ in (3 cm)

¾ in (2 cm)

Back shoulder strap

Stitch three times to hold in place

Back (right side)

Pass the elastic through the opening

⅝ in (1.5 cm)

Overlay by ¾ in (2 cm)

Stitch three times

Elastic

49

pattern II
no darts

cape-collar blouse

Fabric

Fabric [Liberty print Tana lawn]: W 43¼ in x L 94½ in (110 cm x 240 cm)
*If your fabric has a one-way print, be sure the pattern pieces are aligned
   in the same direction.
Buttons: ⅜ in (1 cm) diameter x 8

Instructions

1 Sew the shoulders of the cape collar (overlock or zigzag the seam allowance on both
   pieces at the same time. Turn the seam allowance toward the back).
2 Sew the edges of the cape collar with a threefold hem (see p. 39) (except at the
   edge you are attaching to the bodice).
3 Sew the bodice shoulders (overlock or zigzag the seam allowance on both pieces at
   the same time. Turn the seam allowance toward the back).
4 Sew the sides (overlock or zigzag the seam allowance on both pieces at the same
   time. Turn the seam allowance toward the back).
5 Fold the facing and edge-stitch the hem. Stitch the innermost edge of the facing.
6 Make a threefold hem.
7 Finish the armholes with the bias binding (using the same fabric as for the bodice)
   (see pp. 40–41).
8 Attach the neckline to the cape collar, and pipe the neckline with the bias binding
   (using the same fabric as for the bodice) (see pp. 40–41).
9 Make the buttonholes and attach the buttons.

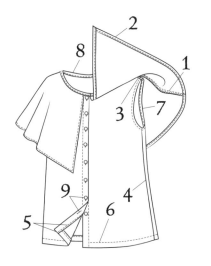

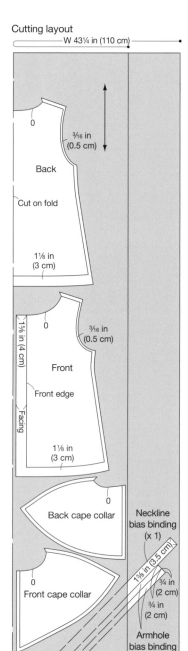

Cutting layout
W 43¼ in (110 cm)

Back
Cut on fold
3/16 in (0.5 cm)
1⅛ in (3 cm)

Front
Front edge
Facing
1⅝ in (4 cm)
3/16 in (0.5 cm)
1⅛ in (3 cm)

Back cape collar

Neckline bias binding (x 1)

Front cape collar
1⅜ in (3.5 cm)
¾ in (2 cm)
¾ in (2 cm)

Armhole bias binding (x 2)

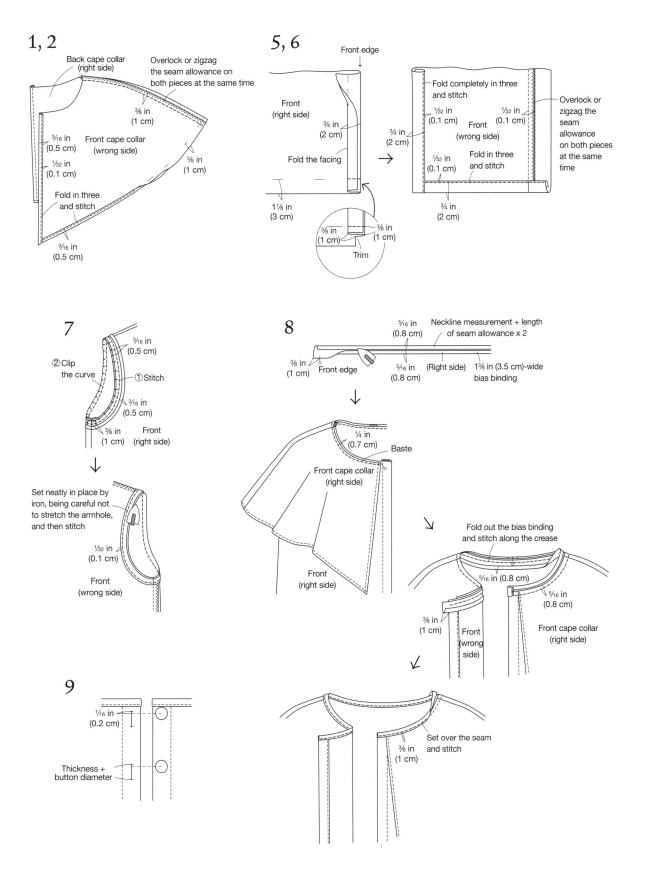

1, 2

Back cape collar (right side)

Overlock or zigzag the seam allowance on both pieces at the same time

Front cape collar (wrong side)

3/8 in (1 cm)

3/16 in (0.5 cm)

1/32 in (0.1 cm)

3/8 in (1 cm)

Fold in three and stitch

3/16 in (0.5 cm)

5, 6

Front edge

Front (right side)

3/4 in (2 cm)

Fold the facing

1 1/8 in (3 cm)

3/8 in (1 cm)

3/8 in (1 cm)

Trim

Fold completely in three and stitch

1/32 in (0.1 cm)

1/32 in (0.1 cm)

3/4 in (2 cm)

Front (wrong side)

Overlock or zigzag the seam allowance on both pieces at the same time

1/32 in (0.1 cm)

Fold in three and stitch

3/4 in (2 cm)

7

② Clip the curve

3/16 in (0.5 cm)

① Stitch

3/16 in (0.5 cm)

3/8 in (1 cm)

Front (right side)

Set neatly in place by iron, being careful not to stretch the armhole, and then stitch

1/32 in (0.1 cm)

Front (wrong side)

8

5/16 in (0.8 cm)

Neckline measurement + length of seam allowance x 2

3/8 in (1 cm)

Front edge

5/16 in (0.8 cm)

(Right side)

1 3/8 in (3.5 cm)-wide bias binding

1/4 in (0.7 cm)

Baste

Front cape collar (right side)

Front (right side)

Fold out the bias binding and stitch along the crease

5/16 in (0.8 cm)

5/16 in (0.8 cm)

3/8 in (1 cm)

Front (wrong side)

Front cape collar (right side)

Set over the seam and stitch

3/8 in (1 cm)

9

1/16 in (0.2 cm)

Thickness + button diameter

pattern II
no darts

tunic with neck ruffle

Fabric

Fabric [cotton Liberty print]: W 43¼ in x L 98⅜ in (110 cm x 250 cm)

*If your fabric has a one-way print, be sure the pattern pieces are aligned in the same direction.

Instructions

1 Sew the edges of the collar ruffles with a threefold hem (see p. 39) (excluding the edge that you are attaching to the bodice), and then sew a gathering stitch in two rows on the edge that is going to be attached. Attach the collar ruffles to the neckline (see p. 45, steps 1 to 3).

2 Sew the shoulders (overlock or zigzag the seam allowance on both pieces at the same time. Turn the seam allowance toward the back).

3 Gather the front neckline and, sandwiching the neckline ruffles, pipe the neckline with the bias binding (using the same fabric as for the bodice) (see pp. 40–41).

4 Sew the sides (overlock or zigzag the seam allowance on both pieces at the same time. Turn the seam allowance toward the back).

5 Make a threefold hem.

6 Sew the sleeve seams (overlock or zigzag the seam allowance on both pieces at the same time. Turn the seam allowance toward the back).

7 Gather the cuffs and pipe them with the bias binding (using the same fabric as for the bodice) (see pp. 40–41).

8 Attach the sleeves (overlock or zigzag the seam allowance on both pieces at the same time. Turn the seam allowances toward the sleeves).

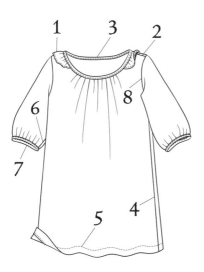

Cutting layout

W 43¼ in (110 cm)

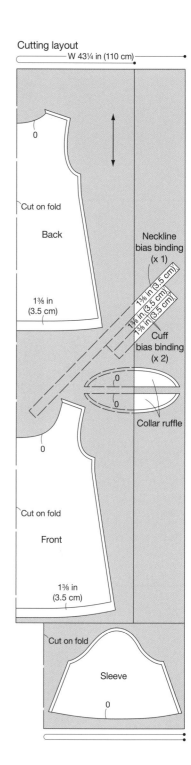

Back

1⅜ in (3.5 cm)

Cut on fold

Neckline bias binding (x 1)

1⅜ in (3.5 cm)
1⅜ in (3.5 cm)
1⅜ in (3.5 cm)
1⅜ in (3.5 cm)

Cuff bias binding (x 2)

Collar ruffle

Cut on fold

Front

1⅜ in (3.5 cm)

Cut on fold

Sleeve

1

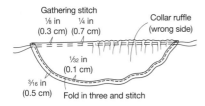

Gathering stitch
⅛ in (0.3 cm) ¼ in (0.7 cm)

Collar ruffle (wrong side)

1/32 in (0.1 cm)

3/16 in (0.5 cm) Fold in three and stitch

3

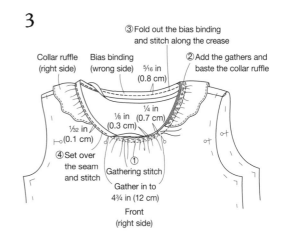

③ Fold out the bias binding and stitch along the crease

Collar ruffle (right side)   Bias binding (wrong side)   5/16 in (0.8 cm)

② Add the gathers and baste the collar ruffle

¼ in (0.7 cm)
⅛ in (0.3 cm)

1/32 in (0.1 cm)

④ Set over the seam and stitch

① Gathering stitch

Gather in to 4¾ in (12 cm)

Front (right side)

5

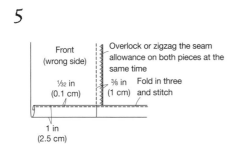

Front (wrong side)

Overlock or zigzag the seam allowance on both pieces at the same time

1/32 in (0.1 cm)   ⅜ in (1 cm)   Fold in three and stitch

1 in (2.5 cm)

6

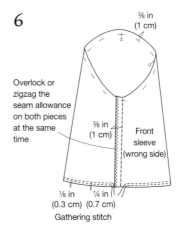

⅜ in (1 cm)

Overlock or zigzag the seam allowance on both pieces at the same time

⅜ in (1 cm)

Front sleeve (wrong side)

⅛ in (0.3 cm)   ¼ in (0.7 cm)

Gathering stitch

7

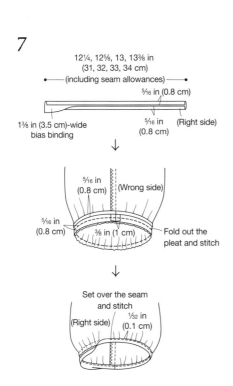

12¼, 12⅝, 13, 13⅜ in
(31, 32, 33, 34 cm)
—(including seam allowances)—

5/16 in (0.8 cm)

1⅜ in (3.5 cm)-wide bias binding

5/16 in (0.8 cm)   (Right side)

↓

5/16 in (0.8 cm)   (Wrong side)

5/16 in (0.8 cm)

⅜ in (1 cm)   Fold out the pleat and stitch

↓

Set over the seam and stitch

(Right side)   1/32 in (0.1 cm)

8

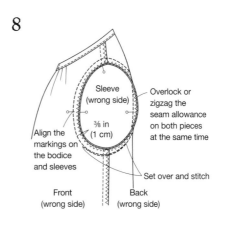

Sleeve (wrong side)

Overlock or zigzag the seam allowance on both pieces at the same time

⅜ in (1 cm)

Align the markings on the bodice and sleeves

Set over and stitch

Front (wrong side)   Back (wrong side)

pattern II
no darts

blouse with shirred flowers

Fabric
Fabric [linen voile]: W 43¼ in x L 98⅜ in (110 cm x 250 cm)
Button: ½ in (1.3 cm) diameter x 1

Instructions
Preparation: Overlock or zigzag the seam allowance on the center back of the bodice.

1 Sew the center back, leaving an opening (press open the seam allowance).
2 Finish the opening (sew with a threefold hem, see p. 39).
3 Sew the shoulders (overlock or zigzag the seam allowance on both pieces at the same time. Turn the seam allowance toward the back).
4 Make the fabric loop.
5 Sandwiching the fabric loop, finish the neckline with the bias binding (using the same fabric as for the bodice) (see pp. 40–41).
6 Attach the ruffles to the neckline and then stitch the rolled ruffles onto the left front bodice.
7 Attach the sleeves (overlock or zigzag the seam allowance on both pieces at the same time. Turn only the seam allowance of the sleeve caps toward the sleeves).
8 Sew the sides and sleeve seams (overlock or zigzag the seam allowance on both pieces at the same time. Turn the seam allowance toward the back).
9 Sew the cuffs with a threefold hem.
10 Make a threefold hem.
11 Sew the ruffles onto the hem and cuffs.
12 Attach the buttons.

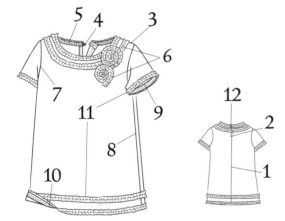

Cutting layout
W 43¼ in (110 cm)

Neckline ruffle (upper)
Neckline ruffle (lower)
Hem ruffle (upper)
Hem ruffle (lower)
Cuff ruffle
Bodice ruffle (upper)
Bodice ruffle (lower)

* None of the ruffles have a seam allowance

Make the ruffle to the full length and trim it to size

1⅛ in (3 cm) each

³⁄₁₆ in (0.5 cm)

¾ in (2 cm)

Back

¾ in (2 cm)

Neckline bias binding (x 1)

¾ in (2 cm)

Fabric loop (x 1)

1⅛ in (3 cm)

1⅛ in (3 cm)

Cut on fold

Front

³⁄₁₆ in (0.5 cm)

Sleeve
1 in (2.5 cm)

1 in (2.5 cm)

Sleeve

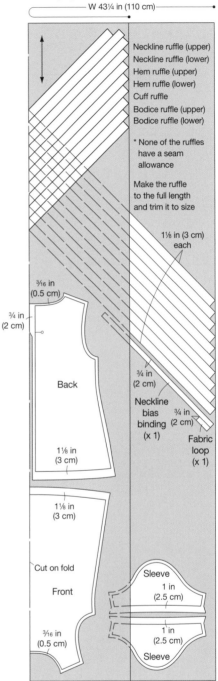

Pattern
Bodice ruffle (upper) x 1
47¼ in (120 cm)

1⅛ in (3 cm)

Bodice ruffle lower x 1
39⅜ in (100 cm)

1⅛ in (3 cm)

How to make the fabric loop

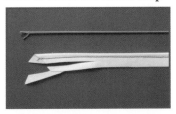

1 Fold the bias binding in two, wrong side out, sew in a width of ⅛ in (0.3 cm), and then trim the seam allowance to ¹⁄₁₆ in (0.2 cm). The photograph shows a looper (top).

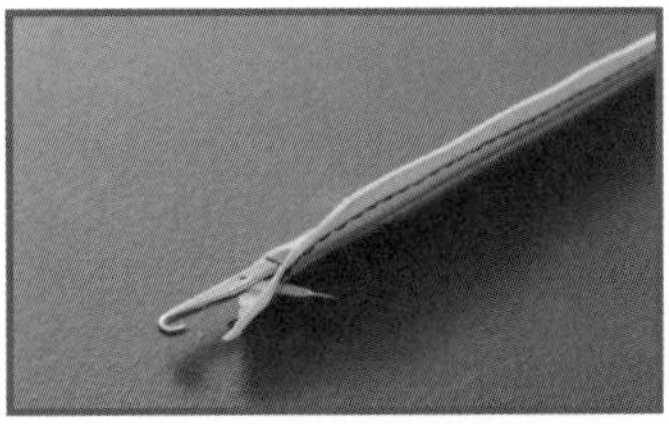

2 Push the looper into the tube formed by the fabric, and hook the claw part onto the seam allowance of the edge.

3 Pull the looper through.

4 Pulling the looper all the way through, turn the fabric right side out. Trim to the specified length.

*Your fabric loop will turn out more neatly if you make it longer than you need and then trim it down to the required size.

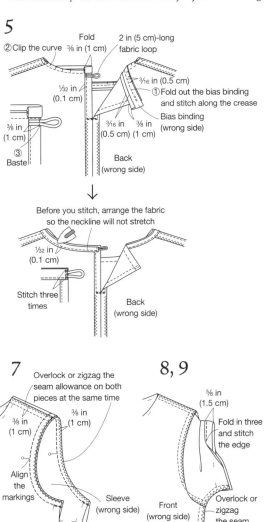

5
② Clip the curve ⅜ in (1 cm) Fold
2 in (5 cm)-long fabric loop
¹⁄₃₂ in (0.1 cm)
³⁄₁₆ in (0.5 cm)
① Fold out the bias binding and stitch along the crease
Bias binding (wrong side)
³⁄₁₆ in (0.5 cm) ⅜ in (1 cm)
⅜ in (1 cm)
③ Baste
Back (wrong side)

Before you stitch, arrange the fabric so the neckline will not stretch
¹⁄₃₂ in (0.1 cm)
Stitch three times
Back (wrong side)

7
Overlock or zigzag the seam allowance on both pieces at the same time
⅜ in (1 cm)
⅜ in (1 cm)
Align the markings
Sleeve (wrong side)
Front (wrong side)

8, 9
⅝ in (1.5 cm)
Fold in three and stitch the edge
Front (wrong side)
Overlock or zigzag the seam allowance on both pieces at the same time
⅜ in (1 cm)

6 Gather the ruffle in from 47¼ to 11¾ in (120 to 30 cm) and roll
◄— 3½ in (9 cm) —►
Gathering stitch
Bodice ruffle (upper)

Gather the ruffle in from 39⅜ to 9⅞ in (100 to 25 cm) and roll
◄— 3⅛ in (8 cm) —►
Bodice ruffle (lower)

Tucking the edge of the start of the ruffle slightly underneath, fold the rest of the ruffle over itself and stitch without overlapping. Roll from the outside to the center

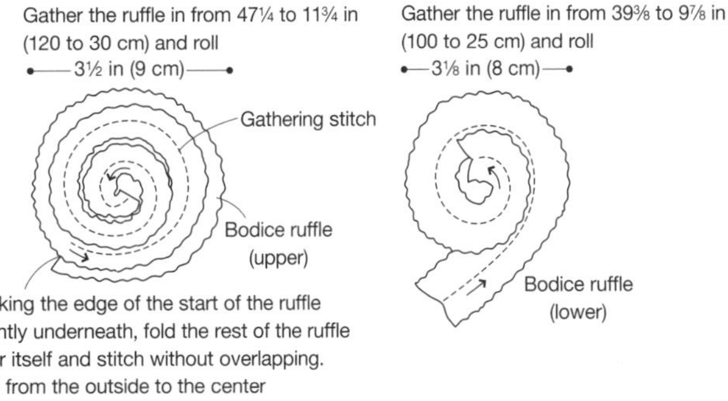

6, 10, 11
⅜ in (1 cm)
1⅛ in (3 cm)
⅜ in (1 cm)
Join both the cuff ruffles and hem ruffles into loops
Sew gathering stitches in two rows
(Right side)

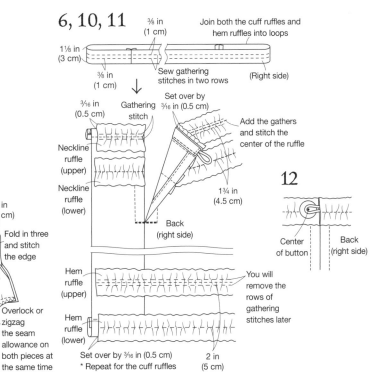

³⁄₁₆ in (0.5 cm)
Gathering stitch
Set over by ³⁄₁₆ in (0.5 cm)
Add the gathers and stitch the center of the ruffle
Neckline ruffle (upper)
Neckline ruffle (lower)
1¾ in (4.5 cm)
Back (right side)
Hem ruffle (upper)
Hem ruffle (lower)
Set over by ³⁄₁₆ in (0.5 cm)
* Repeat for the cuff ruffles
2 in (5 cm)
You will remove the rows of gathering stitches later

12
Center of button
Back (right side)

page 15

pattern **II**
no darts

empire-bodice shift

Fabric

Fabric [cotton voile print]: W 43¼ in x L 137⅞ in
(110 cm x 350 cm)

*If your fabric has a one-way print, be sure the
pattern pieces are aligned in the same direction.

Stay tape (for the front edge): W⅜ in x L 19⅝ in
(1 cm x 50 cm)

Instructions

Preparation: Attach the stay tape to the front edge.

1 Sew the shoulders (overlock or zigzag the seam
   allowance on both pieces at the same time. Turn
   the seam allowance toward the back).
2 Sew the sides of the bodice (overlock or zigzag
   the seam allowance on both pieces at the same
   time. Turn the seam allowance toward the back).
3 Sew the front edge with a threefold hem (see
   p. 39).
4 Pipe the neckline with the bias binding (using the
   same fabric as for the bodice) (see pp. 40–41).
5 Sew the sides of the skirt (overlock or zigzag the
   seam allowance on both pieces at the same time.
   Turn the seam allowance toward the back), and
   gather the waist.
6 Make a threefold hem.
7 Sew the bodice and skirt together (overlock or
   zigzag the seam allowance on both pieces at
   the same time. Turn the seam allowance toward
   the bodice).
8 Sew the sleeve seams (overlock or zigzag the
   seam allowance on both pieces at the same time.
   Turn the seam allowance toward the back).
9 Sew the cuffs with a threefold hem.
10 Attach the sleeves (overlock or zigzag the seam
   allowance on both pieces at the same time.
   Turn the seam allowance toward the sleeves)
   (see p. 53).

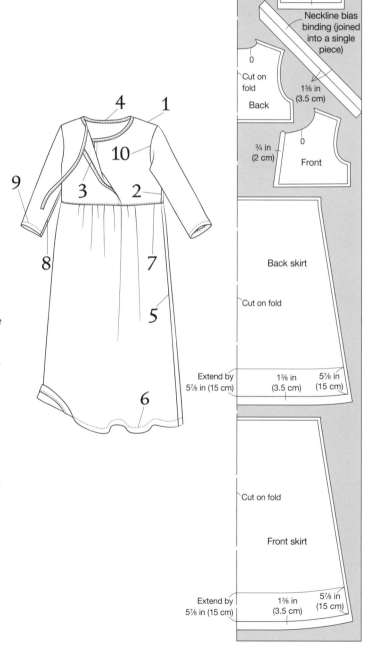

Cutting layout

W 43¼ in (110 cm)

Sleeve

1 in
(2.5 cm)

Neckline bias
binding (joined
into a single
piece)

0

Cut on
fold

Back

1⅜ in
(3.5 cm)

¾ in
(2 cm)

0

Front

Back skirt

Cut on fold

Extend by
5⅞ in (15 cm)

1⅜ in
(3.5 cm)

5⅞ in
(15 cm)

Cut on fold

Front skirt

Extend by
5⅞ in (15 cm)

1⅜ in
(3.5 cm)

5⅞ in
(15 cm)

1 to 3

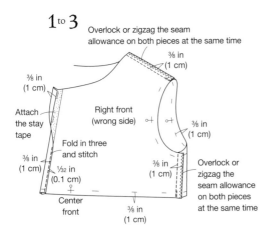

Overlock or zigzag the seam allowance on both pieces at the same time

³⁄₈ in (1 cm)

³⁄₈ in (1 cm)

Attach the stay tape

Right front (wrong side)

³⁄₈ in (1 cm)

Fold in three and stitch

³⁄₈ in (1 cm)

½₂ in (0.1 cm)

Center front

³⁄₈ in (1 cm)

³⁄₈ in (1 cm)

Overlock or zigzag the seam allowance on both pieces at the same time

4

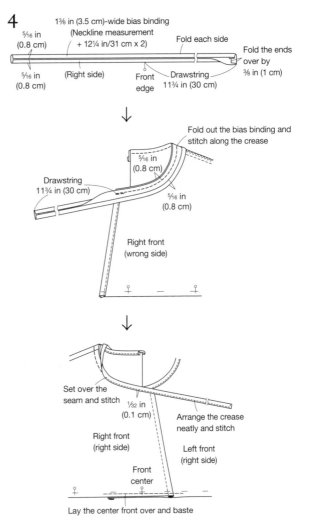

1⅜ in (3.5 cm)-wide bias binding
(Neckline measurement + 12¼ in/31 cm x 2)

Fold each side

⁵⁄₁₆ in (0.8 cm)

⁵⁄₁₆ in (0.8 cm)

(Right side)

Front edge

Drawstring 11¾ in (30 cm)

Fold the ends over by ³⁄₈ in (1 cm)

Fold out the bias binding and stitch along the crease

⁵⁄₁₆ in (0.8 cm)

Drawstring 11¾ in (30 cm)

⁵⁄₁₆ in (0.8 cm)

Right front (wrong side)

Set over the seam and stitch

½₂ in (0.1 cm)

Arrange the crease neatly and stitch

Right front (right side)

Left front (right side)

Front center

Lay the center front over and baste

5, 6

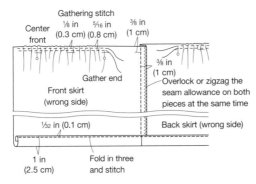

Center front

Gathering stitch

⅛ in (0.3 cm)

⁵⁄₁₆ in (0.8 cm)

³⁄₈ in (1 cm)

³⁄₈ in (1 cm)

Gather end

Overlock or zigzag the seam allowance on both pieces at the same time

Front skirt (wrong side)

½₂ in (0.1 cm)

Back skirt (wrong side)

1 in (2.5 cm)

Fold in three and stitch

7

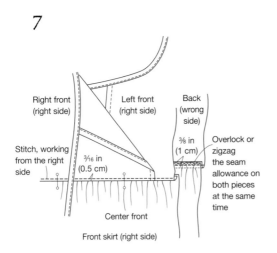

Right front (right side)

Left front (right side)

Back (wrong side)

³⁄₁₆ in (0.5 cm)

³⁄₈ in (1 cm)

Overlock or zigzag the seam allowance on both pieces at the same time

Stitch, working from the right side

Center front

Front skirt (right side)

8, 9

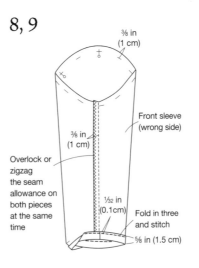

³⁄₈ in (1 cm)

Front sleeve (wrong side)

³⁄₈ in (1 cm)

Overlock or zigzag the seam allowance on both pieces at the same time

½₂ in (0.1cm)

Fold in three and stitch

⅝ in (1.5 cm)

page
16

pattern III
straight-cut

button-front kimono

Fabric

Fabric [cotton gauze]: W 44⅞ in x L 98⅜ in (114 cm x 250 cm)
Lace: W approx. 2 in x L 118⅛ in (5 cm x 300 cm)
Buttons: ⅝ in (1.5 cm) diameter x 5

Instructions

1 Sandwich the lace between the neckline and the bias binding (using the same fabric as for the bodice) (see pp. 40–41).
2 Fold up the facing and edge-stitch the hem.
3 Stitch the innermost edge of the facing.
4 Make a threefold hem (see p. 39).
5 Gather the bodice and sew on the sleeves (overlock or zigzag the seam allowance on both pieces at the same time. Turn the seam allowance toward the sleeves).
6 Sew the sleeve seams and sides (overlock or zigzag the seam allowance on both pieces at the same time. Turn the seam allowance toward the back).
7 Sew the cuffs with a threefold hem.
8 Attach the lace to the hem.
9 Make the buttonholes and attach the buttons.

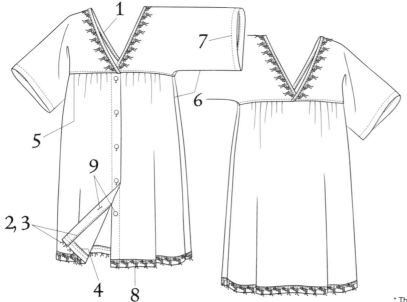

Cutting layout

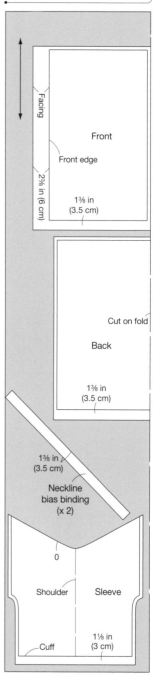

— W 44⅞ in (114 cm) —

Facing

Front

Front edge

2⅜ in (6 cm)

1⅜ in (3.5 cm)

Cut on fold

Back

1⅜ in (3.5 cm)

1⅜ in (3.5 cm)

Neckline bias binding (x 2)

0

Shoulder   Sleeve

Cuff

1⅛ in (3 cm)

* The full-scale pattern piece is for the sleeves only

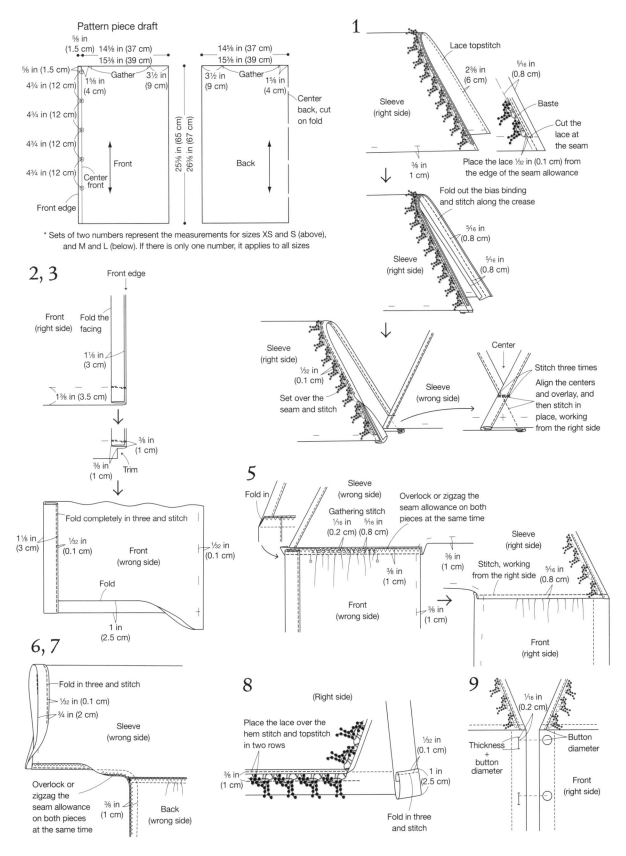

page 20

pattern III
straight-cut

kimono tunic

Fabric
Fabric [voile check]: W 44⅛ in x L 74¾ in (112 cm x 190 cm)
*If your fabric has a large, one-way print repeat and you want to match it up, be sure to buy at least 20 in (50 cm) extra.

Instructions
Preparation: Overlock or zigzag the seam allowance on the bodice.
1. Sew the center front and back of the sleeves as far as the opening of the collar (press open the seam allowance).
2. Sew the neckline with a threefold hem (see p. 39).
3. Sew the cuffs with a threefold hem.
4. Sew the sides of the bodice (press open the seam allowance).
5. Make a threefold hem.
6. Gather the bodice and sew on the sleeves (overlock or zigzag the seam allowance on both pieces at the same time as far as the cuffs. Turn the seam allowance toward the sleeves).
7. Fold the slits in the sleeve seams in two, and stitch as far as the cuffs on the left and right.

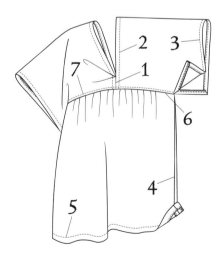

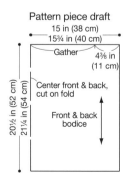

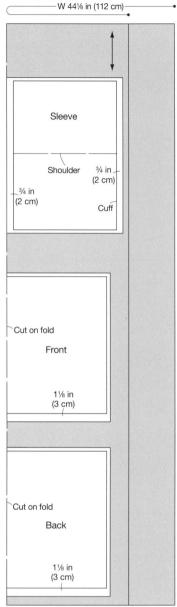

Cutting layout

W 44⅛ in (112 cm)

Sleeve

Shoulder — ¾ in (2 cm)

¾ in (2 cm)

Cuff

Cut on fold
Front
1⅛ in (3 cm)

Cut on fold
Back
1⅛ in (3 cm)

* All pattern piece drafts

Pattern piece draft

15 in (38 cm)
15¾ in (40 cm)
Gather
4⅜ in (11 cm)
Center front & back, cut on fold
20½ in (52 cm)
21¼ in (54 cm)
Front & back bodice

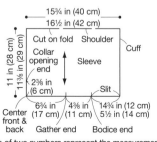

15¾ in (40 cm)
16½ in (42 cm)
Cut on fold   Shoulder
Cuff
Collar opening end
Sleeve
11 in (28 cm)
11⅜ in (29 cm)
2⅜ in (6 cm)
Slit
Center front & back
6¾ in (17 cm)
Gather end
4⅜ in (11 cm)
Bodice end
14¾ in (12 cm)
5½ in (14 cm)

*Sets of two numbers represent the measurements for sizes XS and S (above), and M and L (below)

1

Back sleeve
(wrong side)

7

Front sleeve
(wrong side)

Collar opening end

¾ in
(2 cm)

2¾ in
(7 cm)

⅜ in
(1 cm)

2

⅜ in
(1 cm)

⅜ in
(1 cm)

Back sleeve
(wrong side)

Neckline

Front sleeve
(wrong side)

Collar opening end

Stitch three
times

Fold in three
and stitch

¹⁄₃₂ in
(0.1 cm)

3

¹⁄₃₂ in
(0.1 cm)

Fold in three
and stitch

Sleeve
(wrong side)

⅜ in
(1 cm)

Slit

⅜ in
(1 cm)

4

Gathering stitch
¹⁄₁₆ in   ⁵⁄₁₆ in
(0.2 cm) (0.8 cm)

⅜ in
(1 cm)

Back
(right side)

Stitch in place on
the finishing line

Front
(wrong side)

⅜ in
(1 cm)

Open

5

Front
(wrong side)

¹⁄₃₂ in
(0.1 cm)

Fold in three
and stitch

¾ in
(2 cm)

6

Overlock or zigzag the seam
allowance on both pieces at
the same time

⅜ in
(1 cm)

Side

Slit

Stitch in place
at the side

Front
(wrong side)

Sleeve
(right
side)

Back
(right side)

7

⁵⁄₁₆ in
(0.8 cm)

Sleeve
(wrong side)

Fold up the hem and
stitch, working from
the right side

⅜ in
(1 cm)

Front
(wrong side)

⁵⁄₁₆ in
(0.8 cm)

Back
(right side)

→

Sleeve
(right side)

Sleeve
(right side)

Stitch three times
on the stitch end

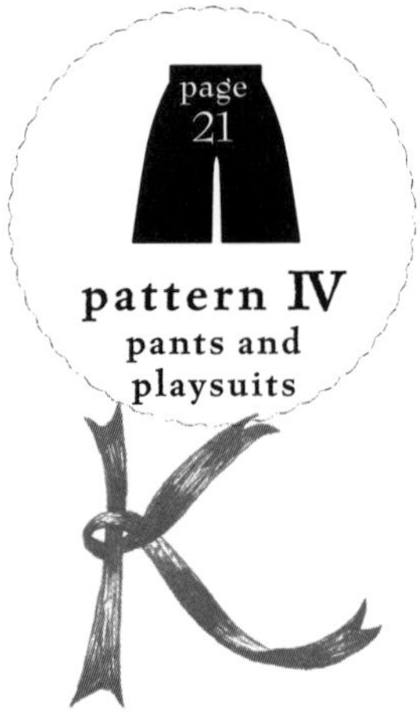
page
21
pattern IV
pants and
playsuits
K

flared pants

Fabric

Fabric [georgette]: W 44⅛ in x L 82⅝ in (112 cm x 210 cm)
Fabric [lining] (for the pettipants/bloomers): W 37 in x L 59⅛ in (94 cm x 150 cm)
Elastic: 8 cord x L 76¾, 82⅝, 88⅝, or 94 4/8 in (195, 210, 225, or 240 cm) (Enough for three strips, including seam allowances. For the flared pants)
W ⅝ in x L 25⅝, 27⅝, 29½, or 31½ in (1.5 cm x 65, 70, 75, or 80 cm) (Including seam allowances. For the pettipants)

Instructions

(For both the flared pants and the pettipants)

1 Sew the sides (overlock or zigzag the seam allowance on both pieces at the same time. Turn the seam allowance toward the back).
2 Sew the inseams (overlock or zigzag the seam allowance on both pieces at the same time. Turn the seam allowance toward the back).
3 Make a threefold hem (see p. 39).
4 Sew the rise, leaving an opening for the elastic in the center back of the waist (overlock or zigzag the seam allowance on both pieces at the same time. Turn the seam allowance toward the right).
5 Sew the waist with a threefold hem and pass the elastic through the opening(s).

Cutting layout [georgette]

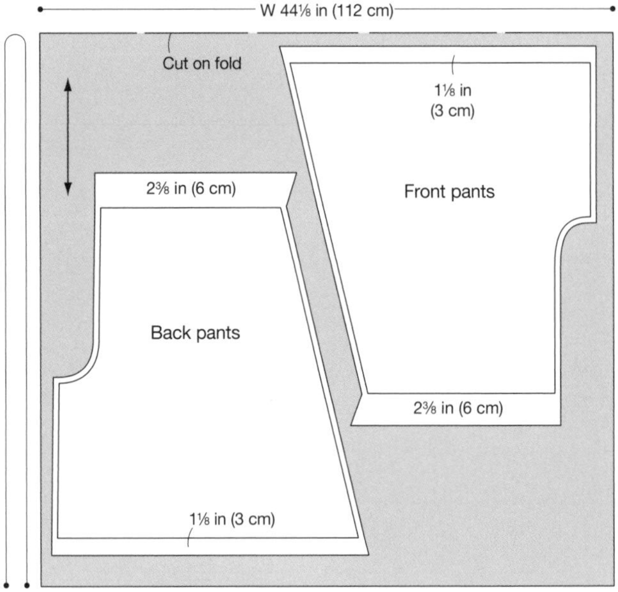
W 44⅛ in (112 cm)
Cut on fold
1⅛ in
(3 cm)
Front pants
2⅜ in (6 cm)
Back pants
2⅜ in (6 cm)
1⅛ in (3 cm)

Cutting layout [lining]

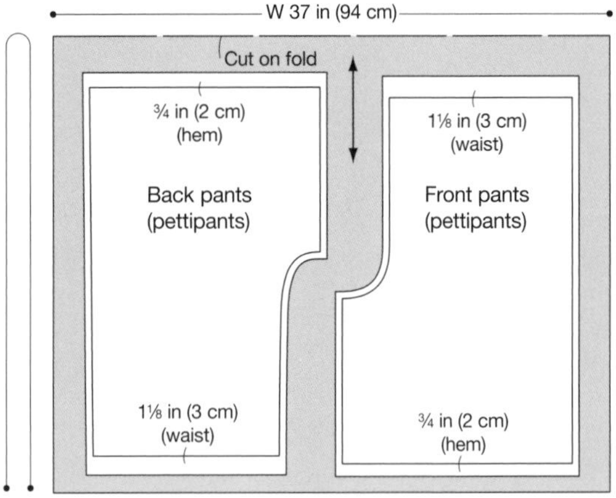
W 37 in (94 cm)
Cut on fold
¾ in (2 cm)
(hem)
Back pants
(pettipants)
1⅛ in (3 cm)
(waist)
1⅛ in (3 cm)
(waist)
Front pants
(pettipants)
¾ in (2 cm)
(hem)

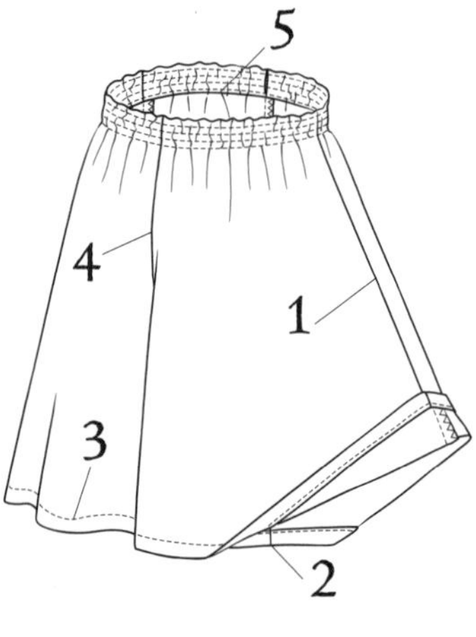
5
4
1
3
2

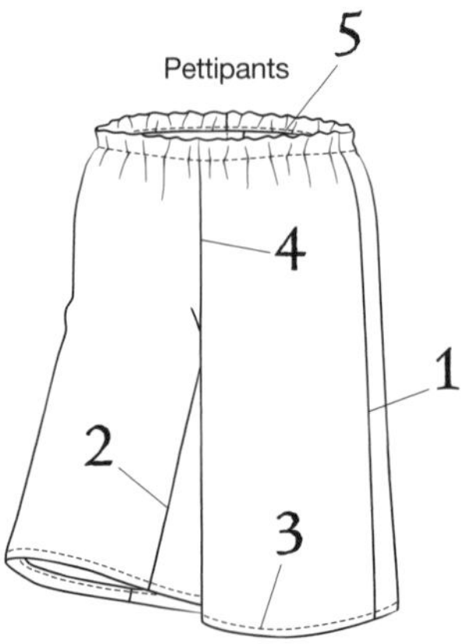
Pettipants
5
4
1
2
3

1

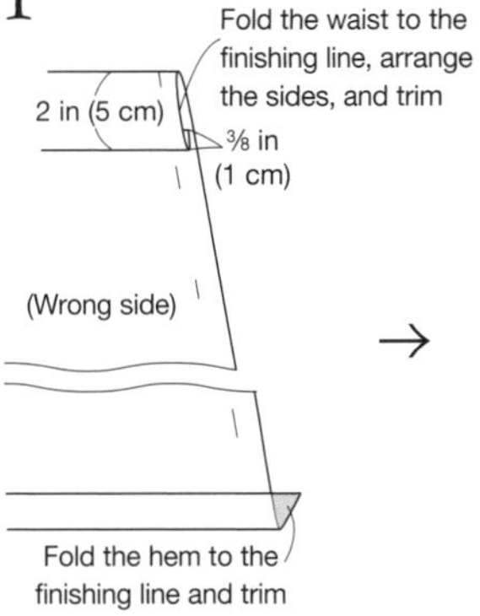
Fold the waist to the finishing line, arrange the sides, and trim
2 in (5 cm)
⅜ in (1 cm)
(Wrong side)
Fold the hem to the finishing line and trim

→

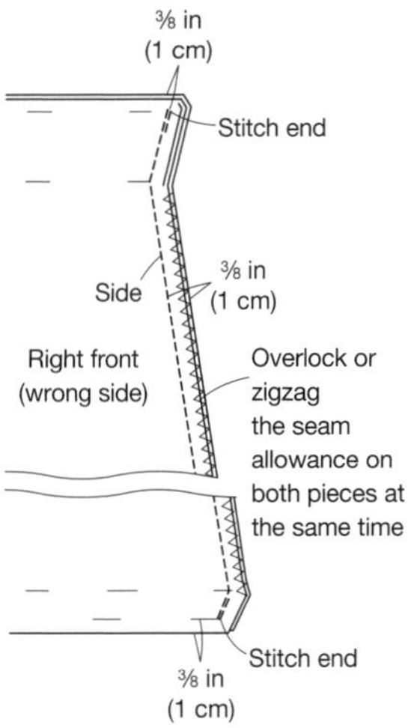
⅜ in (1 cm)
Stitch end
Side
⅜ in (1 cm)
Right front (wrong side)
Overlock or zigzag the seam allowance on both pieces at the same time
Stitch end
⅜ in (1 cm)

2, 3

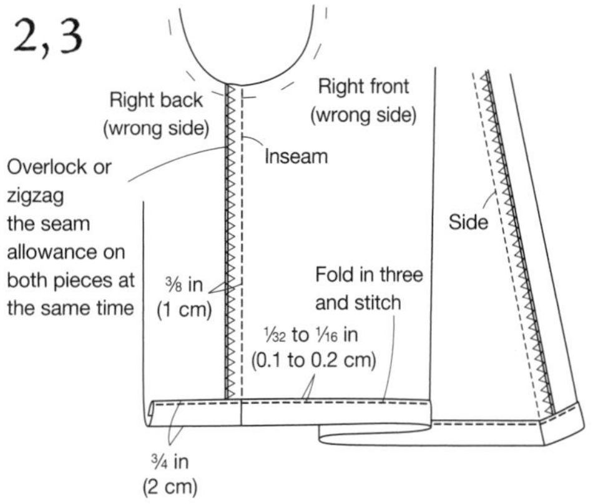
Right back (wrong side)
Right front (wrong side)
Overlock or zigzag the seam allowance on both pieces at the same time
Inseam
Side
⅜ in (1 cm)
Fold in three and stitch
1⁄32 to 1⁄16 in (0.1 to 0.2 cm)
¾ in (2 cm)

4

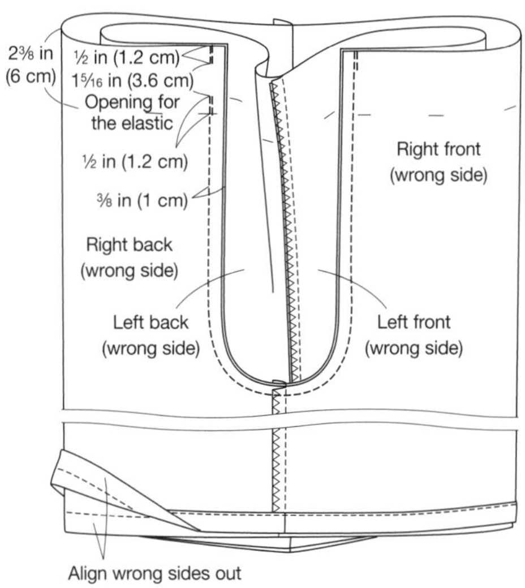
2⅜ in (6 cm)
½ in (1.2 cm)
1 5⁄16 in (3.6 cm)
Opening for the elastic
½ in (1.2 cm)
⅜ in (1 cm)
Right front (wrong side)
Right back (wrong side)
Left back (wrong side)
Left front (wrong side)
Align wrong sides out

→

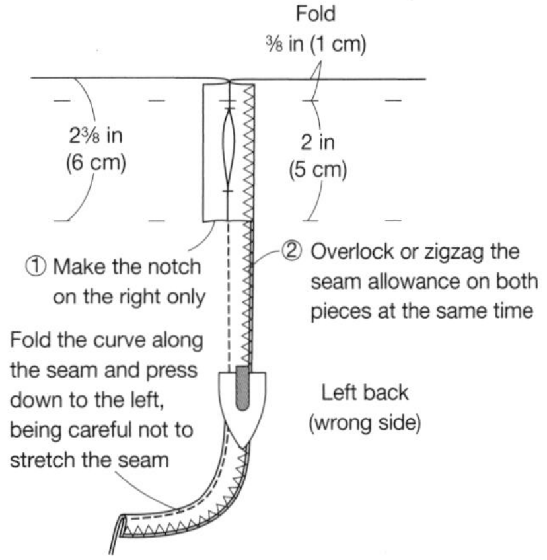
Fold
⅜ in (1 cm)
2⅜ in (6 cm)
2 in (5 cm)
① Make the notch on the right only
② Overlock or zigzag the seam allowance on both pieces at the same time
Fold the curve along the seam and press down to the left, being careful not to stretch the seam
Left back (wrong side)

5

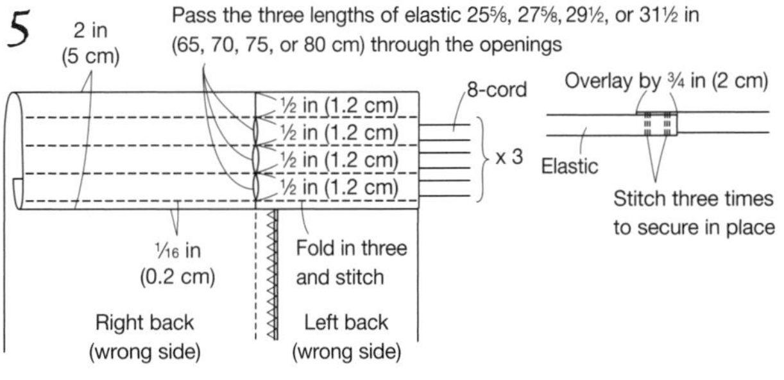
2 in (5 cm)
Pass the three lengths of elastic 25⅝, 27⅝, 29½, or 31½ in (65, 70, 75, or 80 cm) through the openings
8-cord
Overlay by ¾ in (2 cm)
½ in (1.2 cm)
½ in (1.2 cm)
½ in (1.2 cm)
½ in (1.2 cm)
x 3
Elastic
Stitch three times to secure in place
1⁄16 in (0.2 cm)
Fold in three and stitch
Right back (wrong side)
Left back (wrong side)

Pettipants

3

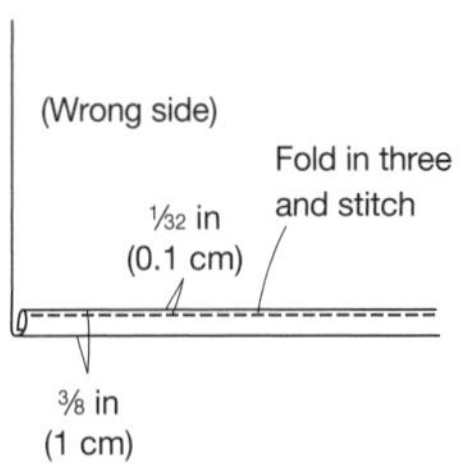
(Wrong side)
Fold in three and stitch
1⁄32 in (0.1 cm)
⅜ in (1 cm)

4

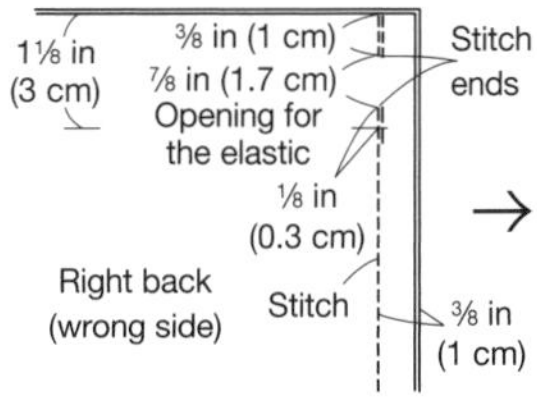
1⅛ in (3 cm)
⅜ in (1 cm)
⅞ in (1.7 cm)
Opening for the elastic
Stitch ends
⅛ in (0.3 cm)
Right back (wrong side)
Stitch
⅜ in (1 cm)

→

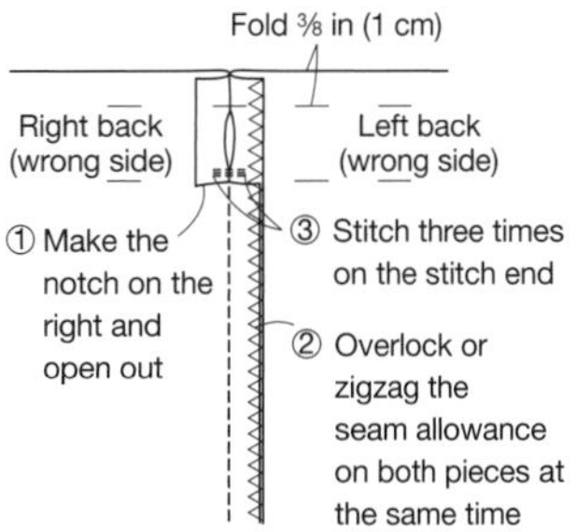
Fold ⅜ in (1 cm)
Right back (wrong side)
Left back (wrong side)
① Make the notch on the right and open out
③ Stitch three times on the stitch end
② Overlock or zigzag the seam allowance on both pieces at the same time

5

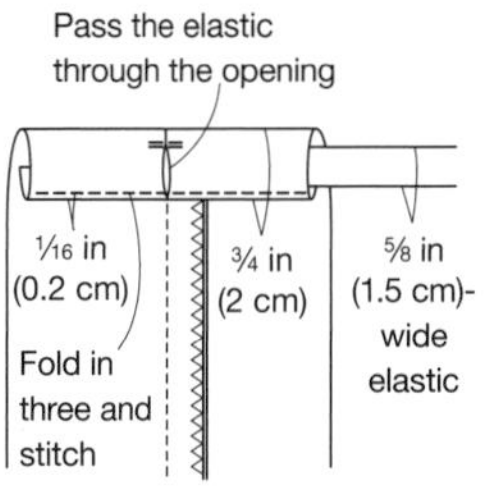
Pass the elastic through the opening
1⁄16 in (0.2 cm)
¾ in (2 cm)
⅝ in (1.5 cm)-wide elastic
Fold in three and stitch

pattern IV
pants and
playsuits

playsuit with tied straps

Fabric

Fabric [cotton Liberty print]: W 43¼ in x L 66⅞ in
  (110 cm x 170 cm)
Elastic: 12 cord x L 25⅝, 27⅝, 29½, or 31½ in (65,
  70, 75, or 80 cm) (including the seam allowance)
Elastic sewing thread: 1 reel

Instructions

1 Sew the sides (overlock or zigzag the seam
   allowance on both pieces at the same time. Turn
   the seam allowance toward the back).
2 Sew the inseams (overlock or zigzag the seam
   allowance on both pieces at the same time. Turn
   the seam allowance toward the back).
3 Make a threefold hem (see p. 39).
4 Sew the rise, leaving an opening for the elastic
   in the top edge of the center back (overlock or
   zigzag the seam allowance on both pieces at the
   same time. Turn the seam allowance toward the
   right).
5 Sew the top edge with a threefold hem.
6 Add the elastic shirring.
7 Make and attach the shoulder straps.
8 Pass the elastic through the opening.

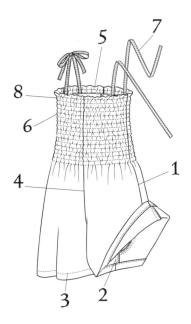

Cutting layout

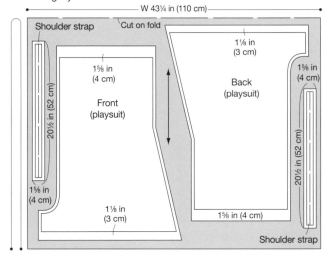

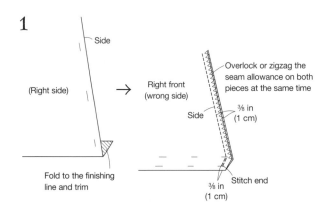

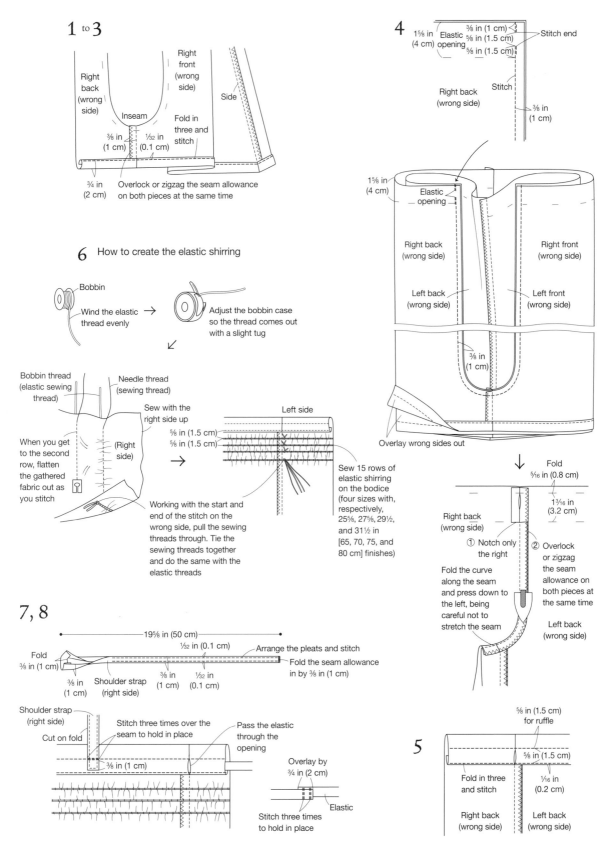

1 to 3

Right back (wrong side)

Right front (wrong side)

Side

Inseam

Fold in three and stitch

³⁄₈ in (1 cm)

¹⁄₃₂ in (0.1 cm)

¾ in (2 cm)

Overlock or zigzag the seam allowance on both pieces at the same time

4

1⅝ in (4 cm)

Elastic opening

³⁄₈ in (1 cm)

⅝ in (1.5 cm)

⅝ in (1.5 cm)

Stitch end

Stitch

Right back (wrong side)

³⁄₈ in (1 cm)

1⅝ in (4 cm)

Elastic opening

Right back (wrong side)

Left back (wrong side)

Right front (wrong side)

Left front (wrong side)

³⁄₈ in (1 cm)

Overlay wrong sides out

Fold
⁵⁄₁₆ in (0.8 cm)

1³⁄₁₆ in (3.2 cm)

Right back (wrong side)

① Notch only the right

② Overlock or zigzag the seam allowance on both pieces at the same time

Fold the curve along the seam and press down to the left, being careful not to stretch the seam

Left back (wrong side)

6 How to create the elastic shirring

Bobbin

Wind the elastic thread evenly →

Adjust the bobbin case so the thread comes out with a slight tug

↙

Bobbin thread (elastic sewing thread)

Needle thread (sewing thread)

Sew with the right side up

(Right side)

When you get to the second row, flatten the gathered fabric out as you stitch

⅝ in (1.5 cm)
⅝ in (1.5 cm)

Left side

→

Working with the start and end of the stitch on the wrong side, pull the sewing threads through. Tie the sewing threads together and do the same with the elastic threads

Sew 15 rows of elastic shirring on the bodice (four sizes with, respectively, 25⅝, 27⅝, 29½, and 31½ in [65, 70, 75, and 80 cm] finishes)

7, 8

19⅝ in (50 cm)

¹⁄₃₂ in (0.1 cm)

Arrange the pleats and stitch

Fold ³⁄₈ in (1 cm)

Fold the seam allowance in by ³⁄₈ in (1 cm)

³⁄₈ in (1 cm)

Shoulder strap (right side)

³⁄₈ in (1 cm)

¹⁄₃₂ in (0.1 cm)

Shoulder strap (right side)

Cut on fold

Stitch three times over the seam to hold in place

³⁄₈ in (1 cm)

Pass the elastic through the opening

Overlay by ¾ in (2 cm)

Elastic

Stitch three times to hold in place

5

⅝ in (1.5 cm) for ruffle

⅝ in (1.5 cm)

Fold in three and stitch

¹⁄₁₆ in (0.2 cm)

Right back (wrong side)

Left back (wrong side)

page
23

pattern IV
pants and
playsuits

strapless jumpsuit

Fabric

Fabric [voile check]: W 45⅝ in x L 114⅛ in
(116 cm x 290 cm)

Elastic: 12 cord x L 25⅝, 27⅝, 29½, or 31½ in
(65, 70, 75, or 80 cm) (including the seam
allowance)

Elastic sewing thread: 1 reel

Instructions

See pp. 64 and 65 for all instructions, but omit the
shoulder straps.

Cutting layout

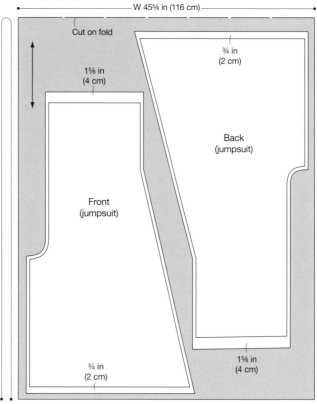

W 45⅝ in (116 cm)

Cut on fold

¾ in (2 cm)

1⅝ in (4 cm)

Back (jumpsuit)

Front (jumpsuit)

¾ in (2 cm)

1⅝ in (4 cm)

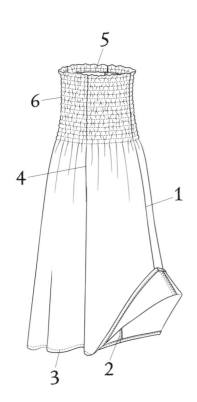

1 to 3

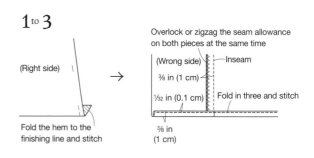

(Right side)

Fold the hem to the finishing line and stitch

→

Overlock or zigzag the seam allowance on both pieces at the same time

(Wrong side) — Inseam

⅜ in (1 cm)

1/32 in (0.1 cm)

Fold in three and stitch

⅜ in (1 cm)

pattern VI
with darts

puff-sleeve shift

Fabric

Fabric [linen]: W 55⅛ in x L 94⅛ in (140 cm x 240 cm)
Fusible interfacing (for the facing): W 3⅞ in x L 5⅞ in (10 cm x 15 cm)
Stay tape (for the zipper opening): W ⅝ in x L 39⅜ in (1.5 cm x 100 cm)
Invisible zipper: 20½ in (52 cm)
Hook and eye x 1
Fabric [lining] (for the petticoat): W 37 in x L 67 in (94 cm x 170 cm) for sizes
    XS and S; or 74¾ in (190 cm) for sizes M and L
Elastic (for the petticoat): W⅜ in x L 23½, 25⅝, 27⅝, or 29½ in (1 cm x 60, 65,
    70, or 75 cm) (including the seam allowance)

Instructions for dress

Preparation: Attach the fusible interfacing to the facing. Attach the fusible stay
    tape to the seam allowance of the zipper opening. Overlock or zigzag the
    seam allowance on the center back, around the pocket, and on the facing.

1 Sew the center back as far as the end of the opening (press open the seam
    allowance). Attach the invisible zipper.
2 Sew the bodice darts.
3 Make and attach the pockets.
4 Finish the opening in the center front with the facing.
5 Sew the shoulders.
6 Gather the front neckline and pipe with the bias binding (using the same
    fabric as for the bodice) (see pp. 40–41).
7 Sew the sides (overlock or zigzag the seam allowance on both pieces at the
    same time. Turn the seam allowance toward the back).
8 Make a threefold hem (see p. 39).
9 Sew the sleeve seams (overlock or zigzag the seam allowance on both
    pieces at the same time. Turn the seam allowance toward the back).
10 Gather the cuffs and pipe them with the bias binding (using the same fabric
    as for the bodice) (see pp. 40–41).
11 Attach the sleeves (overlock or zigzag the seam allowance on both pieces
    at the same time. Turn the seam allowance toward the sleeves) (see p. 53).
12 Attach the hook and eye.
13 Make the ribbon in the same fabric as the bodice.

Instructions for petticoat

1 Sew the sides, leaving an opening for the elastic to pass through (overlock
    or zigzag the seam allowance on both pieces at the same time. Turn the
    seam allowance to one side).
2 Sew the waist with a threefold hem (see p. 39) and pass the elastic through
    the opening.
3 Attach the hem ruffle (overlock or zigzag the seam allowance on both
    pieces at the same time. Turn the seam allowance toward the skirt).

Cutting layout

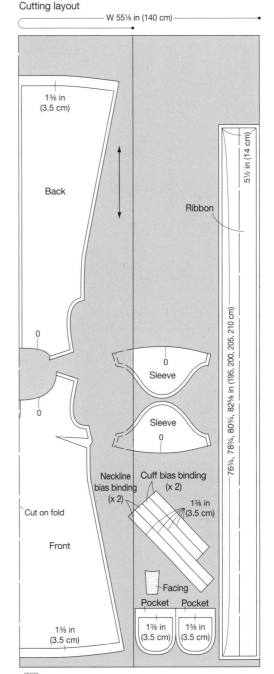

* ▦ Fusible interfacing

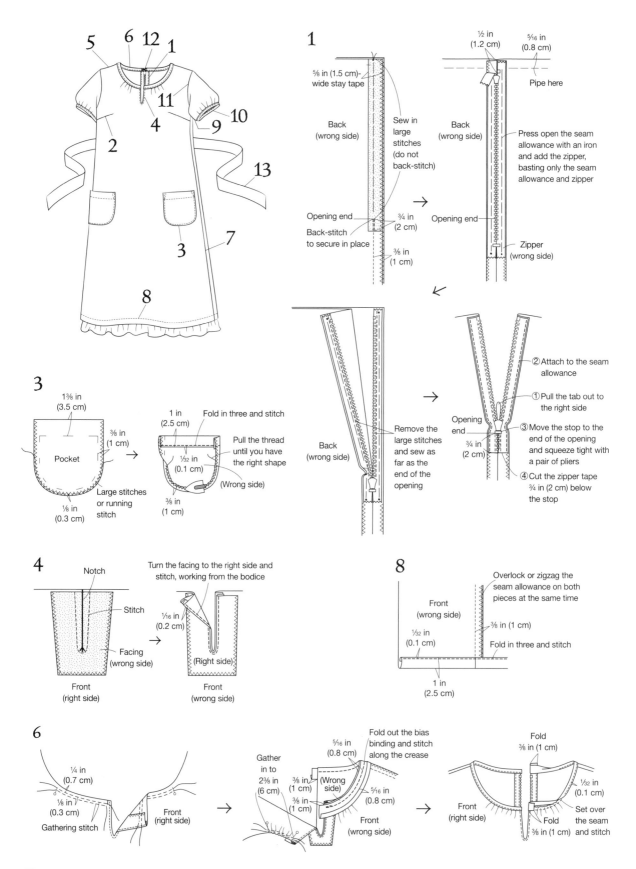

5 6 12 1

11

4

2

10

9

13

7

3

8

1

⅝ in (1.5 cm)-wide stay tape

Back (wrong side)

Sew in large stitches (do not back-stitch)

Opening end

Back-stitch to secure in place

¾ in (2 cm)

⅜ in (1 cm)

½ in (1.2 cm)

⁵⁄₁₆ in (0.8 cm)

Pipe here

Back (wrong side)

Press open the seam allowance with an iron and add the zipper, basting only the seam allowance and zipper

Opening end

Zipper (wrong side)

Back (wrong side)

Remove the large stitches and sew as far as the end of the opening

Opening end

¾ in (2 cm)

② Attach to the seam allowance

① Pull the tab out to the right side

③ Move the stop to the end of the opening and squeeze tight with a pair of pliers

④ Cut the zipper tape ¾ in (2 cm) below the stop

3

1⅜ in (3.5 cm)

⅜ in (1 cm)

Pocket

⅛ in (0.3 cm)

Large stitches or running stitch

1 in (2.5 cm)

Fold in three and stitch

Pull the thread until you have the right shape

(Wrong side)

1⁄32 in (0.1 cm)

⅜ in (1 cm)

4

Notch

Stitch

Facing (wrong side)

Front (right side)

Turn the facing to the right side and stitch, working from the bodice

1⁄16 in (0.2 cm)

(Right side)

Front (wrong side)

8

Front (wrong side)

1⁄32 in (0.1 cm)

Overlock or zigzag the seam allowance on both pieces at the same time

⅜ in (1 cm)

Fold in three and stitch

1 in (2.5 cm)

6

¼ in (0.7 cm)

⅛ in (0.3 cm)

Gathering stitch

Front (right side)

Gather in to 2⅜ in (6 cm)

⁵⁄₁₆ in (0.8 cm)

Fold out the bias binding and stitch along the crease

⅜ in (1 cm)

(Wrong side)

⅜ in (1 cm)

⁵⁄₁₆ in (0.8 cm)

Front (wrong side)

Fold ⅜ in (1 cm)

Front (right side)

1⁄32 in (0.1 cm)

Fold

Set over the seam and stitch

⅜ in (1 cm)

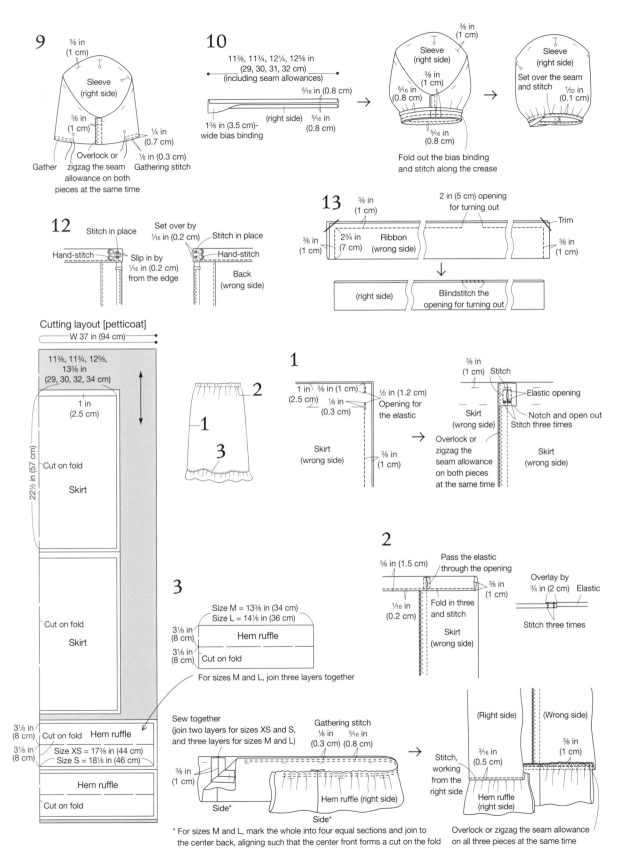

9

⅜ in (1 cm)

Sleeve (right side)

⅜ in (1 cm)

¼ in (0.7 cm)

⅛ in (0.3 cm)
Gathering stitch

Gather   Overlock or zigzag the seam allowance on both pieces at the same time

10

11⅜, 11¾, 12¼, 12⅝ in (29, 30, 31, 32 cm) (including seam allowances)

5⁄16 in (0.8 cm)

1⅜ in (3.5 cm)-wide bias binding   (right side)   5⁄16 in (0.8 cm)

⅜ in (1 cm)

Sleeve (right side)

⅜ in (1 cm)

5⁄16 in (0.8 cm)

5⁄16 in (0.8 cm)

Fold out the bias binding and stitch along the crease

Sleeve (right side)

Set over the seam and stitch   1⁄32 in (0.1 cm)

12

Stitch in place

Hand-stitch

Set over by 1⁄16 in (0.2 cm)   Stitch in place

Slip in by 1⁄16 in (0.2 cm) from the edge   Hand-stitch

Back (wrong side)

13

⅜ in (1 cm)   2 in (5 cm) opening for turning out   Trim

⅜ in (1 cm)   2¾ in (7 cm)   Ribbon (wrong side)   ⅜ in (1 cm)

(right side)   Blindstitch the opening for turning out

Cutting layout [petticoat]

W 37 in (94 cm)

11⅜, 11¾, 12⅝, 13⅜ in (29, 30, 32, 34 cm)

1 in (2.5 cm)

22½ in (57 cm)

Cut on fold

Skirt

Cut on fold

Skirt

3⅛ in (8 cm)   Cut on fold   Hem ruffle
3⅛ in (8 cm)   Size XS = 17⅜ in (44 cm)   Size S = 18⅛ in (46 cm)

Hem ruffle

Cut on fold

1

2

3

1

1 in (2.5 cm)   ⅜ in (1 cm)   ½ in (1.2 cm) Opening for the elastic
⅛ in (0.3 cm)

Skirt (wrong side)

⅜ in (1 cm)

⅜ in (1 cm)   Stitch   Elastic opening

Skirt (wrong side)   Notch and open out
Stitch three times

Overlock or zigzag the seam allowance on both pieces at the same time

Skirt (wrong side)

2

⅝ in (1.5 cm)   Pass the elastic through the opening   ⅜ in (1 cm)

1⁄16 in (0.2 cm)   Fold in three and stitch

Skirt (wrong side)

Overlay by ¾ in (2 cm)   Elastic

Stitch three times

3

Size M = 13⅜ in (34 cm)
Size L = 14⅛ in (36 cm)

3⅛ in (8 cm)   Hem ruffle

3⅛ in (8 cm)   Cut on fold

For sizes M and L, join three layers together

Sew together (join two layers for sizes XS and S, and three layers for sizes M and L)

Gathering stitch
⅛ in (0.3 cm)   5⁄16 in (0.8 cm)

⅜ in (1 cm)

Side*   Side*

Hem ruffle (right side)

* For sizes M and L, mark the whole into four equal sections and join to the center back, aligning such that the center front forms a cut on the fold

(Right side)   (Wrong side)

⅜ in (1 cm)

Stitch, working from the right side

3⁄16 in (0.5 cm)

Hem ruffle (right side)

Overlock or zigzag the seam allowance on all three pieces at the same time

page 25

pattern V
raglan sleeve

tie-neck camisole

Fabric
Fabric [Antares chambray]: W 55⅛ in x L 51⅛ in (140 cm x 130 cm)
Fabric [tulle]: W 74¾ in x L 27⅝ in (190 cm x 70 cm)
Fusible interfacing (for the right- and wrong-side yokes):
    W 35⅜ in x L 11¾ in (90 cm x 30 cm)

Instructions
Preparation: Attach the fusible interfacing to the right- and wrong-side
    yokes, both front and back.

1 Sew the sides of the bodice (overlock or zigzag the seam allowance
   on both pieces at the same time. Turn the seam allowance toward
   the back). Sew the sides of the tulle (leaving no seam allowance on
   the hem).
2 Make a threefold hem on the bodice (see p. 39).
3 Gather the bodice and tulle separately, overlay the tulle on the right
   side, and baste the seam allowance in place.
4 Finish the armholes with the bias binding (using the same fabric as
   for the bodice) (see pp. 40–41).
5 Edge-stitch the front and back yokes separately. Fold out the
   shoulders of the right- and wrong-side yokes (front and back),
   and then align them wrong sides out and sew (opening the seam
   allowance). Blindstitch the outside of the shoulder part of the yokes.
6 Sew together the bodice and wrong-side yoke (turning the seam
   allowance toward the yoke). Lay over the right-side yoke and stitch.
7 Make the ribbon and sew it onto the left shoulder.

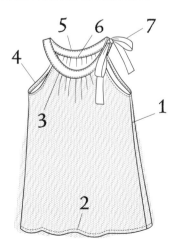

Cutting layout [Antares chambray]

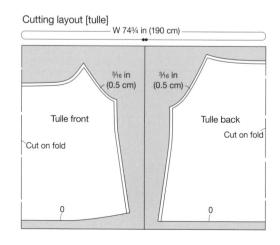

W 55⅛ in (140 cm)

Right side
back yoke

Cut on fold   ³⁄₁₆ in (0.5 cm)

Wrong side
back yoke

¾ in (2 cm)

Back

Cut on fold

Right side
front yoke

³⁄₁₆ in (0.5 cm)   ³⁄₁₆ in (0.5 cm)

³⁄₁₆ in (0.5 cm)

Cut on fold   Wrong side front yoke

³⁄₁₆ in (0.5 cm)

1⅜ in (3.5 cm)

39⅜ in (100 cm)

¾ in (2 cm)   Ribbon

Front

Armhole bias binding (x 2)

Cut on fold   ¾ in (2 cm)

Fusible interfacing

Cutting layout [tulle]

W 74¾ in (190 cm)

³⁄₁₆ in (0.5 cm)   ³⁄₁₆ in (0.5 cm)

Tulle front   Tulle back

Cut on fold   Cut on fold

0   0

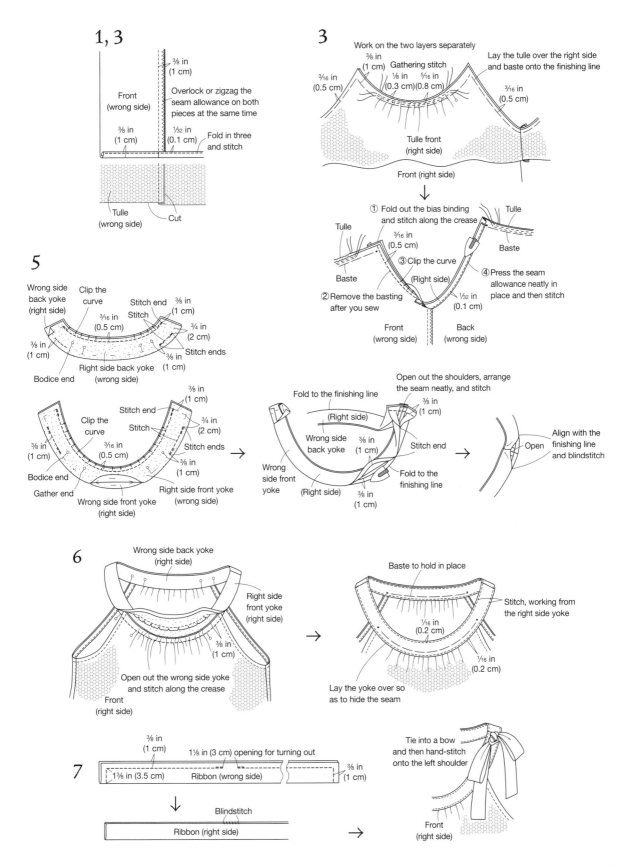

1, 3

⅜ in (1 cm)

Front (wrong side)

Overlock or zigzag the seam allowance on both pieces at the same time

⅜ in (1 cm)   ¹⁄₃₂ in (0.1 cm)

Fold in three and stitch

Tulle (wrong side)

Cut

3

Work on the two layers separately

⅜ in (1 cm)   Gathering stitch

³⁄₁₆ in (0.5 cm)   ⅛ in (0.3 cm)   ⁵⁄₁₆ in (0.8 cm)   ³⁄₁₆ in (0.5 cm)

Lay the tulle over the right side and baste onto the finishing line

Tulle front (right side)

Front (right side)

① Fold out the bias binding and stitch along the crease

Tulle

Tulle   Baste

Baste   ³⁄₁₆ in (0.5 cm)

③ Clip the curve

(Right side)

② Remove the basting after you sew

④ Press the seam allowance neatly in place and then stitch

¹⁄₃₂ in (0.1 cm)

Front (wrong side)   Back (wrong side)

5

Wrong side back yoke (right side)

Clip the curve

Stitch end   Stitch   ⅜ in (1 cm)

³⁄₁₆ in (0.5 cm)   ¾ in (2 cm)

⅜ in (1 cm)   Stitch ends

Bodice end   Right side back yoke (wrong side)   ⅜ in (1 cm)

⅜ in (1 cm)

Stitch end   Stitch   ¾ in (2 cm)

Clip the curve

⅜ in (1 cm)   ³⁄₁₆ in (0.5 cm)   Stitch ends   ⅜ in (1 cm)

Bodice end   Wrong side front yoke (right side)   Right side front yoke (wrong side)

Gather end

→

Fold to the finishing line

(Right side)

Wrong side back yoke   ⅜ in (1 cm)

Wrong side front yoke   (Right side)

Open out the shoulders, arrange the seam neatly, and stitch

⅜ in (1 cm)

Stitch end

Fold to the finishing line

⅜ in (1 cm)

→

Open   Align with the finishing line and blindstitch

6

Wrong side back yoke (right side)

Right side front yoke (right side)

⅜ in (1 cm)

Open out the wrong side yoke and stitch along the crease

Front (right side)

→

Baste to hold in place

Stitch, working from the right side yoke

¹⁄₁₆ in (0.2 cm)

¹⁄₁₆ in (0.2 cm)

Lay the yoke over so as to hide the seam

7

⅜ in (1 cm)

1⅛ in (3 cm) opening for turning out

1⅜ in (3.5 cm)   Ribbon (wrong side)

⅜ in (1 cm)

↓

Blindstitch

Ribbon (right side)

→

Tie into a bow and then hand-stitch onto the left shoulder

Front (right side)

page 26

pattern V
raglan sleeve

tunic dress with draped hem

Fabric

Fabric [cotton check]: W 45⅝ in x L 86⅝ in (116 cm x 220 cm)
*If your fabric has a one-way print, be sure the pattern pieces are aligned in the same direction.

Instructions

1. Make the drawstrings (see p. 55).
2. Make a threefold hem (see p. 39).
3. Sew the cuffs with a threefold hem. Overlock or zigzag the seam allowances of the front sleeve raglan seams and front bodice raglan seams.
4. Align the back bodice and sleeves wrong sides out and sew the back raglan seams (overlock or zigzag the seam allowance on both pieces at the same time. Turn the seam allowances toward the bodice).
5. Finish the neckline section of the back bodice and sleeves with the bias binding (using the same fabric as for the bodice) (see pp. 40–41).
6. Finish the neckline section of the front bodice with the bias binding (using the same fabric as for the bodice) (see pp. 40–41).
7. Align the front bodice and sleeves wrong sides out and sew the front raglan seams (press open the seam allowance). Stitch the drawstring opening, pass the drawstrings through, and stitch in place.
8. After basting down the stay stitch on the open seam allowance with a few stitches, sew the sides (overlock or zigzag the seam allowance on both pieces at the same time. Turn the seam allowance toward the back).

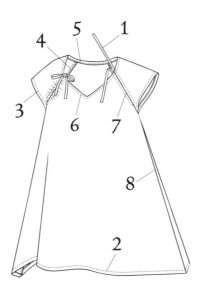

Cutting layout

W 45⅝ in (116 cm)

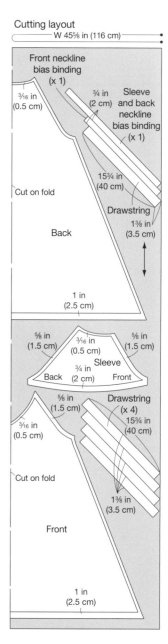

Front neckline bias binding (x 1)

³⁄₁₆ in (0.5 cm)

¾ in (2 cm) Sleeve and back neckline bias binding (x 1)

Cut on fold

15¾ in (40 cm)

Back

Drawstring
1⅜ in (3.5 cm)

1 in (2.5 cm)

⅝ in (1.5 cm)   ³⁄₁₆ in (0.5 cm)   ⅝ in (1.5 cm)

¾ in (2 cm)   Sleeve

Back   Front

⅝ in (1.5 cm)   Drawstring (x 4)

³⁄₁₆ in (0.5 cm)   15¾ in (40 cm)

Cut on fold

1⅜ in (3.5 cm)

Front

1 in (2.5 cm)

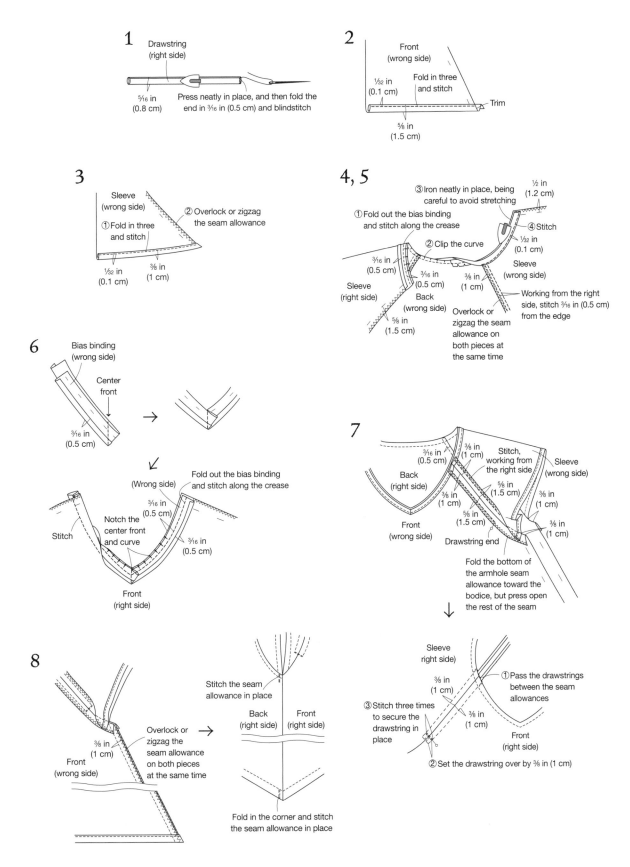

1

Drawstring
(right side)

⁵⁄₁₆ in
(0.8 cm)

Press neatly in place, and then fold the
end in ³⁄₁₆ in (0.5 cm) and blindstitch

2

Front
(wrong side)

¹⁄₃₂ in
(0.1 cm)

Fold in three
and stitch

Trim

⁵⁄₈ in
(1.5 cm)

3

Sleeve
(wrong side)

② Overlock or zigzag
the seam allowance

① Fold in three
and stitch

¹⁄₃₂ in
(0.1 cm)

³⁄₈ in
(1 cm)

4, 5

③ Iron neatly in place, being
careful to avoid stretching

½ in
(1.2 cm)

① Fold out the bias binding
and stitch along the crease

④ Stitch

② Clip the curve

¹⁄₃₂ in
(0.1 cm)

³⁄₁₆ in
(0.5 cm)

³⁄₁₆ in
(0.5 cm)

³⁄₈ in
(1 cm)

Sleeve
(wrong side)

Sleeve
(right side)

Back
(wrong side)

Working from the right
side, stitch ³⁄₁₆ in (0.5 cm)
from the edge

⁵⁄₈ in
(1.5 cm)

Overlock or
zigzag the seam
allowance on
both pieces at
the same time

6

Bias binding
(wrong side)

Center
front

³⁄₁₆ in
(0.5 cm)

→

Fold out the bias binding
and stitch along the crease

(Wrong side)

³⁄₁₆ in
(0.5 cm)

Stitch

Notch the
center front
and curve

³⁄₁₆ in
(0.5 cm)

Front
(right side)

7

³⁄₁₆ in
(0.5 cm)

³⁄₈ in
(1 cm)

Stitch,
working from
the right side

Sleeve
(wrong side)

Back
(right side)

⁵⁄₈ in
(1.5 cm)

³⁄₈ in
(1 cm)

³⁄₈ in
(1 cm)

⁵⁄₈ in
(1.5 cm)

Front
(wrong side)

Drawstring end

³⁄₈ in
(1 cm)

Fold the bottom of
the armhole seam
allowance toward the
bodice, but press open
the rest of the seam

↓

Sleeve
right side)

³⁄₈ in
(1 cm)

① Pass the drawstrings
between the seam
allowances

③ Stitch three times
to secure the
drawstring in
place

³⁄₈ in
(1 cm)

Front
(right side)

② Set the drawstring over by ³⁄₈ in (1 cm)

8

Stitch the seam
allowance in place

Back
(right side)

Front
(right side)

Overlock or
zigzag the seam
allowance
on both pieces
at the same time

→

³⁄₈ in
(1 cm)

Front
(wrong side)

Fold in the corner and stitch
the seam allowance in place

pattern V
raglan sleeve

ruffle-trim coat dress

Fabric

Fabric [Oxford chambray]: W 43¼ in x L 118⅛ in (110 cm x 300 cm)
Buttons: ⅝ in (1.5 cm) diameter x 6

Instructions

1 Make and attach the pockets.
2 Align the bodice and sleeves wrong sides out and sew the front and back raglan seams (overlock or zigzag the seam allowance on both pieces at the same time. Turn the seam allowance toward the bodice).
3 Sew the sides and sleeve seams (overlock or zigzag the seam allowance on both pieces at the same time. Turn the seam allowance toward the back).
4 Sew the cuffs with a threefold hem (see p. 39).
5 Fold up the facing and edge-stitch the hem.
6 Finish the neckline with the bias binding (using the same fabric as for the bodice) (see pp. 40–41).
7 Stitch the innermost edge of the facing.
8 Make a threefold hem.
9 Make the ruffles and sew them onto the neckline and right hem.
10 Make the buttonholes and attach the buttons.

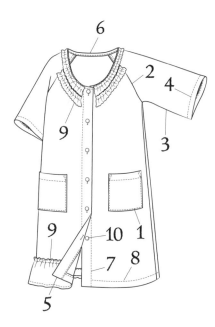

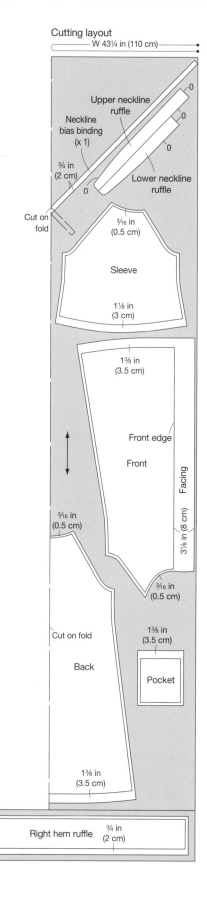

Cutting layout

W 43¼ in (110 cm)

Upper neckline ruffle

Neckline bias binding (x 1)

¾ in (2 cm)

Cut on fold

Lower neckline ruffle

³⁄₁₆ in (0.5 cm)

Sleeve

1⅛ in (3 cm)

1⅜ in (3.5 cm)

Front edge

Front

Facing

3⅛ in (8 cm)

³⁄₁₆ in (0.5 cm)

³⁄₁₆ in (0.5 cm)

Cut on fold

1⅜ in (3.5 cm)

Back

Pocket

1⅜ in (3.5 cm)

Right hem ruffle   ¾ in (2 cm)

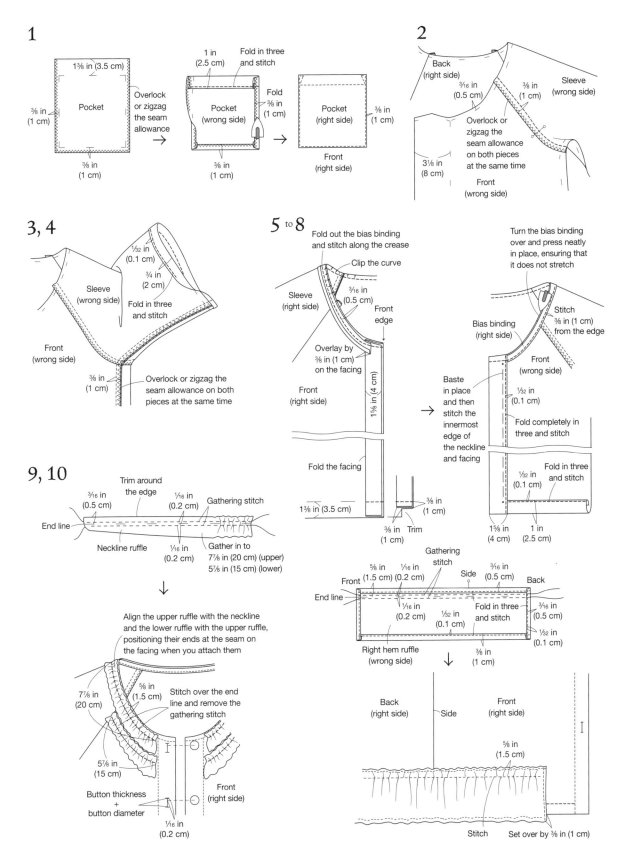

1

1⅜ in (3.5 cm)

⅜ in (1 cm)

Pocket

Overlock or zigzag the seam allowance

→

⅜ in (1 cm)

1 in (2.5 cm)

Fold in three and stitch

Pocket (wrong side)

Fold ⅜ in (1 cm)

⅜ in (1 cm)

→

Pocket (right side)

⅜ in (1 cm)

Front (right side)

2

Back (right side)

³⁄₁₆ in (0.5 cm)

⅜ in (1 cm)

Sleeve (wrong side)

Overlock or zigzag the seam allowance on both pieces at the same time

3⅛ in (8 cm)

Front (wrong side)

3, 4

Sleeve (wrong side)

1⁄32 in (0.1 cm)

¾ in (2 cm)

Fold in three and stitch

Front (wrong side)

⅜ in (1 cm)

Overlock or zigzag the seam allowance on both pieces at the same time

5 to 8

Fold out the bias binding and stitch along the crease

Clip the curve

Sleeve (right side)

³⁄₁₆ in (0.5 cm)

Front edge

Overlay by ⅜ in (1 cm) on the facing

Front (right side)

1⅝ in (4 cm)

Fold the facing

1⅜ in (3.5 cm)

⅜ in (1 cm)   Trim

⅜ in (1 cm)

Turn the bias binding over and press neatly in place, ensuring that it does not stretch

Stitch ⅜ in (1 cm) from the edge

Bias binding (right side)

Baste in place and then stitch the innermost edge of the neckline and facing

→

Front (wrong side)

1⁄32 in (0.1 cm)

Fold completely in three and stitch

1⁄32 in (0.1 cm)

Fold in three and stitch

1⅝ in (4 cm)

1 in (2.5 cm)

9, 10

³⁄₁₆ in (0.5 cm)

Trim around the edge

1⁄16 in (0.2 cm)

Gathering stitch

End line

Neckline ruffle

1⁄16 in (0.2 cm)

Gather in to 7⅞ in (20 cm) (upper) 5⅞ in (15 cm) (lower)

↓

Align the upper ruffle with the neckline and the lower ruffle with the upper ruffle, positioning their ends at the seam on the facing when you attach them

7⅞ in (20 cm)

⅝ in (1.5 cm)

Stitch over the end line and remove the gathering stitch

5⅞ in (15 cm)

Button thickness + button diameter

1⁄16 in (0.2 cm)

Front (right side)

Gathering stitch

⅝ in (1.5 cm)

1⁄16 in (0.2 cm)

Front

End line

1⁄16 in (0.2 cm)

Side

1⁄32 in (0.1 cm)

³⁄₁₆ in (0.5 cm)

Back

Fold in three and stitch

³⁄₁₆ in (0.5 cm)

1⁄32 in (0.1 cm)

Right hem ruffle (wrong side)

⅜ in (1 cm)

↓

Back (right side)

Side

Front (right side)

⅝ in (1.5 cm)

Stitch

Set over by ⅜ in (1 cm)

page
29

pattern V
raglan sleeve

tucked-bodice blouse

Fabric

Fabric [cotton print]: W 44⅛-in x L 98⅜ in (112 cm x 250 cm)

Cotton tape: W ⅜ in x L 27⅝ in (0.9 cm x 70 cm)

Elastic: 8 cord x L 24⅜, 25⅞, 26, or 26⅝ in (62, 64, 66, or 68 cm) (including the seam allowance)

Instructions

1 Sew the tucks in the front bodice (turning them toward the side).
2 Align the bodice and sleeves wrong sides out and sew the front and back raglan seams (overlock or zigzag the seam allowance on both pieces at the same time. Turn the seam allowance toward the bodice).
3 Sew the sleeve seams and sides (overlock or zigzag the seam allowance on both pieces at the same time. Turn the seam allowance toward the back).
4 Sew the cuffs with a threefold hem (see p. 39).
5 Make a threefold hem.
6 Finish the neckline with the bias binding (using the same fabric as for the bodice) (see pp. 40–41).
7 Pass the cotton tape through the neckline. Sew on and tie the cotton tape.

Cutting layout

W 44⅛ in (112 cm)

1⅛ in (3 cm)

Cut on fold

Front

Sew the tucks and re-trim

3⅞ in (10 cm)

1⅛ in (3 cm)

Back

Cut on fold

Neckline bias binding (joined into a single length)

1 in (2.5 cm)

3/16 in (0.5 cm)

Sleeve

3/16 in (0.5 cm)

Sleeve

¾ in (2 cm)

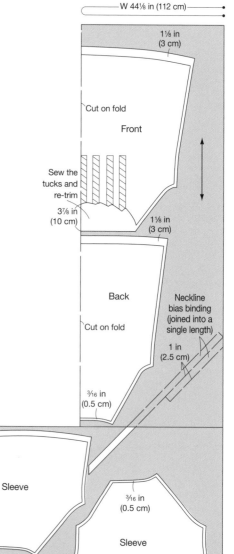

1

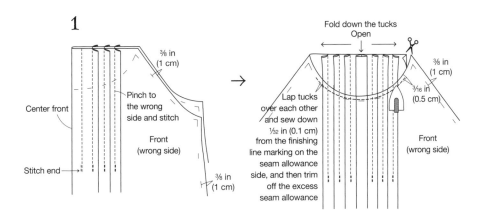

Center front

Pinch to
the wrong
side and stitch

⅜ in
(1 cm)

Front
(wrong side)

Stitch end →

⅜ in
(1 cm)

Fold down the tucks
Open

Lap tucks
over each other
and sew down
1⁄32 in (0.1 cm)
from the finishing
line marking on the
seam allowance
side, and then trim
off the excess
seam allowance

⅜ in
(1 cm)

3⁄16 in
(0.5 cm)

Front
(wrong side)

2

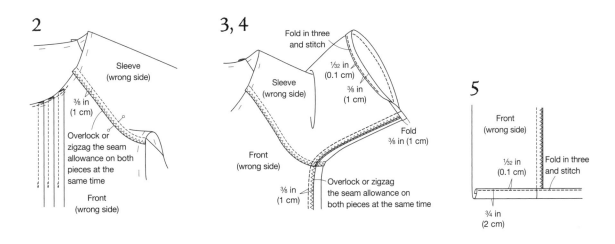

Sleeve
(wrong side)

⅜ in
(1 cm)

Overlock or
zigzag the seam
allowance on both
pieces at the
same time

Front
(wrong side)

3, 4

Fold in three
and stitch

Sleeve
(wrong side)

1⁄32 in
(0.1 cm)

⅜ in
(1 cm)

Front
(wrong side)

Fold
⅜ in (1 cm)

⅜ in
(1 cm)

Overlock or zigzag
the seam allowance on
both pieces at the same time

5

Front
(wrong side)

1⁄32 in
(0.1 cm)

Fold in three
and stitch

¾ in
(2 cm)

6, 7

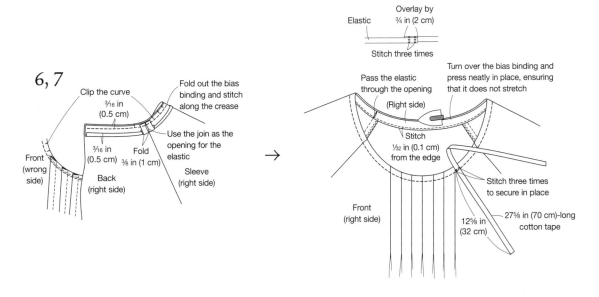

Clip the curve
3⁄16 in
(0.5 cm)

Fold out the bias
binding and stitch
along the crease

Use the join as the
opening for the
elastic

Front
(wrong
side)

3⁄16 in
(0.5 cm)

Fold
⅜ in (1 cm)

Back
(right side)

Sleeve
(right side)

Elastic

Overlay by
¾ in (2 cm)

Stitch three times

Pass the elastic
through the opening

(Right side)

Turn over the bias binding and
press neatly in place, ensuring
that it does not stretch

Stitch
1⁄32 in (0.1 cm)
from the edge

Front
(right side)

Stitch three times
to secure in place

12⅝ in
(32 cm)

27⅝ in (70 cm)-long
cotton tape

page
31

pattern VI
with darts

sweetheart-bodice dress

Fabric

Fabric [cotton Liberty print]: W 43¼ in x L 82⅝ in
   (110 cm x 210 cm)

*If your fabric has a one-way print, be sure the pattern
   pieces are aligned in the same direction.

Fabric [georgette]: W 44⅛ in x L 23⅝ in
   (112 cm x 60 cm)

Button: ½ in (1.3 cm) diameter x 1

Fusible interfacing: 2 in x 2 in (5 cm x 5 cm)

Instructions

Preparation: Overlock or zigzag the seam allowance on
   the center back and sides of the lower bodice back,
   and the sides of the front and back skirts.

1 Attach the fusible interfacing at the position of the slit
   in the lower bodice front. Make the fabric loop (see
   p. 55).

2 Sew the fabric loop onto the center back of the right-
   back bodice upper, and then sew the seam allowance
   with a threefold hem (see p. 39).

3 French-seam the shoulders (turning the seam
   allowance toward the back).

4 Sew the center back of the lower bodice back (press
   open the seam allowance).

5 Sew the bust darts in the lower bodice front (turning
   the darts upward), and then overlock or zigzag the
   seam allowance of the sides.

6 Sew together the seams of the front and back upper
   and lower bodices (overlock or zigzag the seam
   allowance on both pieces at the same time. Turn the
   seam allowance toward the lower bodice).

7 Sew the sides of the lower bodice (press open the
   seam allowance).

8 Bind the neckline and armholes with the bias
   binding (using the same fabric as for the bodice)
   (see pp. 40–41).

9 Sew the sides of the skirt (press open the seam
   allowance).

10 Make a threefold hem.

11 Gather the skirt and sew to the bodice (overlock or
   zigzag the seam allowance on both pieces at the same
   time. Turn the seam allowance toward the bodice).

12 Attach the button.

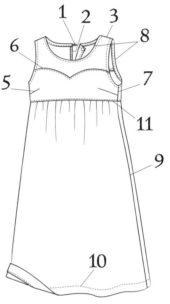

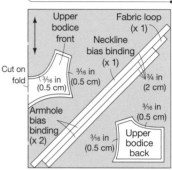

Cutting layout [georgette]

W 44⅛ in (112 cm)

Upper bodice front

Fabric loop (x 1)

Neckline bias binding (x 1)

Cut on fold

³⁄₁₆ in (0.5 cm)

¾ in (2 cm)

³⁄₁₆ in (0.5 cm)

Armhole bias binding (x 2)

³⁄₁₆ in (0.5 cm)

Upper bodice back

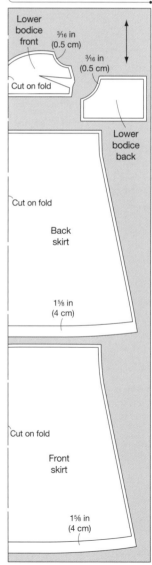

Cutting layout [Liberty print]

W 43¼ in (110 cm)

Lower bodice front

³⁄₁₆ in (0.5 cm)

³⁄₁₆ in (0.5 cm)

Cut on fold

Lower bodice back

Cut on fold

Back skirt

1⅝ in (4 cm)

Cut on fold

Front skirt

1⅝ in (4 cm)

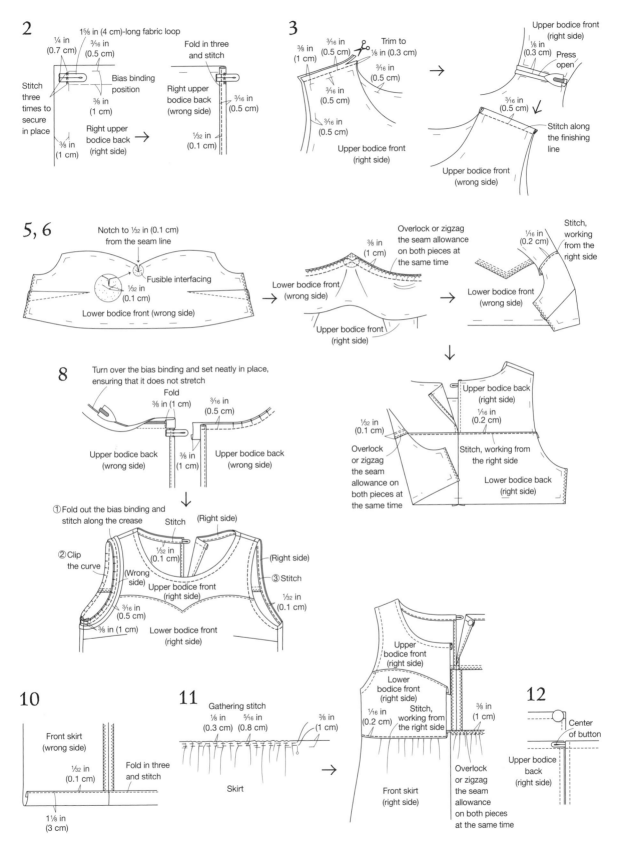

2

¼ in (0.7 cm)

1⅝ in (4 cm)-long fabric loop

³⁄₁₆ in (0.5 cm)

Fold in three and stitch

Stitch three times to secure in place

Bias binding position

³⁄₈ in (1 cm)

Right upper bodice back (wrong side)

³⁄₁₆ in (0.5 cm)

Right upper bodice back (right side)

³⁄₈ in (1 cm)

³⁄₂ in (0.1 cm)

3

³⁄₈ in (1 cm)

³⁄₁₆ in (0.5 cm)

Trim to ⅛ in (0.3 cm)

³⁄₁₆ in (0.5 cm)

³⁄₁₆ in (0.5 cm)

³⁄₁₆ in (0.5 cm)

Upper bodice front (right side)

Upper bodice front (right side)

⅛ in (0.3 cm)

Press open

³⁄₁₆ in (0.5 cm)

Stitch along the finishing line

Upper bodice front (wrong side)

5, 6

Notch to ½₂ in (0.1 cm) from the seam line

Fusible interfacing

½₂ in (0.1 cm)

Lower bodice front (wrong side)

³⁄₈ in (1 cm)

Overlock or zigzag the seam allowance on both pieces at the same time

Lower bodice front (wrong side)

Upper bodice front (right side)

¹⁄₁₆ in (0.2 cm)

Stitch, working from the right side

Lower bodice front (wrong side)

8

Turn over the bias binding and set neatly in place, ensuring that it does not stretch

Fold

³⁄₈ in (1 cm)

³⁄₁₆ in (0.5 cm)

Upper bodice back (wrong side)

³⁄₈ in (1 cm)

Upper bodice back (wrong side)

Upper bodice back (right side)

¹⁄₁₆ in (0.2 cm)

½₂ in (0.1 cm)

Overlock or zigzag the seam allowance on both pieces at the same time

Stitch, working from the right side

Lower bodice back (right side)

① Fold out the bias binding and stitch along the crease

Stitch (Right side)

½₂ in (0.1 cm)

(Right side)

② Clip the curve

(Wrong side)

Upper bodice front (right side)

③ Stitch

½₂ in (0.1 cm)

³⁄₁₆ in (0.5 cm)

³⁄₈ in (1 cm)

Lower bodice front (right side)

10

Front skirt (wrong side)

½₂ in (0.1 cm)

Fold in three and stitch

1⅛ in (3 cm)

11

Gathering stitch

⅛ in (0.3 cm)

⁵⁄₁₆ in (0.8 cm)

³⁄₈ in (1 cm)

Skirt

Upper bodice front (right side)

Lower bodice front (right side)

¹⁄₁₆ in (0.2 cm)

Stitch, working from the right side

³⁄₈ in (1 cm)

Front skirt (right side)

Overlock or zigzag the seam allowance on both pieces at the same time

12

Center of button

Upper bodice back (right side)

pattern VI
with darts

wrap-bodice sleeveless dress

Fabric

Fabric [slub lawn cotton print]: W 43¼ in x L 98⅜ in
(110 cm x 250 cm).

Instructions

1 Sew the bust darts (turning them upward).

2 Sew the shoulders (overlock or zigzag the seam allowance on
   both pieces at the same time. Turn the seam allowance toward
   the back).

3 Sew the sides of the bodice (overlock or zigzag the seam
   allowance on both pieces at the same time. Turn the seam
   allowance toward the back).

4 Finish the armholes with the bias binding (using the same
   fabric as for the bodice) (see pp. 40–41).

5 Finish the neckline with the bias binding (using the same fabric
   as for the bodice) (see pp. 40–41)

6 Finish the overlap at the center front, and then stitch the edges
   of the bodice in place.

7 Sew the sides of the skirt (overlock or zigzag the seam
   allowance on both pieces at the same time. Turn the seam
   allowance toward the back).

8 Make a threefold hem
   (see p. 39).

9 Sew the bodice and skirt
   together (overlock or zigzag
   the seam allowance on both
   pieces at the same time.
   Turn the seam allowance
   toward the skirt).

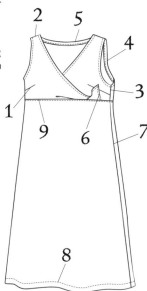

Cutting layout

W 43¼ in (110 cm)

Face side

Back
bodice

³⁄₁₆ in
(0.5 cm)

³⁄₁₆ in
(0.5 cm)

³⁄₁₆ in
(0.5 cm)

Left
bodice
front

Neckline bias binding
(joined into a single length)

Armhole bias
binding
(x 2)

³⁄₁₆ in
(0.5 cm)

Right
bodice
front

¾ in
(2 cm)

Front
skirt

1⅛ in
(3 cm)

Back
skirt

1⅛ in
(3 cm)

4, 5

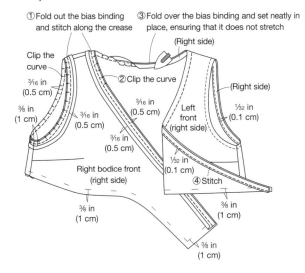

① Fold out the bias binding and stitch along the crease

③ Fold over the bias binding and set neatly in place, ensuring that it does not stretch

(Right side)

Clip the curve

³⁄₁₆ in (0.5 cm)

② Clip the curve

(Right side)

³⁄₈ in (1 cm)

³⁄₁₆ in (0.5 cm)

³⁄₁₆ in (0.5 cm)

Left front (right side)

¹⁄₃₂ in (0.1 cm)

³⁄₁₆ in (0.5 cm)

Right bodice front (right side)

¹⁄₃₂ in (0.1 cm)

④ Stitch

³⁄₈ in (1 cm)

³⁄₈ in (1 cm)

³⁄₈ in (1 cm)

6

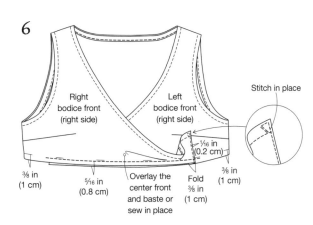

Right bodice front (right side)

Left bodice front (right side)

Stitch in place

¹⁄₁₆ in (0.2 cm)

³⁄₈ in (1 cm)

⁵⁄₁₆ in (0.8 cm)

Overlay the center front and baste or sew in place

Fold ³⁄₈ in (1 cm)

³⁄₈ in (1 cm)

8

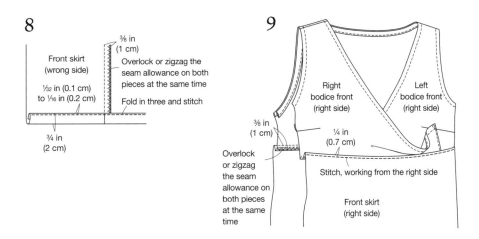

Front skirt (wrong side)

³⁄₈ in (1 cm)

Overlock or zigzag the seam allowance on both pieces at the same time

Fold in three and stitch

¹⁄₃₂ in (0.1 cm) to ¹⁄₁₆ in (0.2 cm)

¾ in (2 cm)

9

Right bodice front (right side)

Left bodice front (right side)

³⁄₈ in (1 cm)

¼ in (0.7 cm)

Overlock or zigzag the seam allowance on both pieces at the same time

Stitch, working from the right side

Front skirt (right side)

page 33

pattern VI
with darts

bishop-sleeve blouse

Fabric

Fabric [cotton jacquard]: W 42½ in x L 86⅝ in
(108 cm x 220 cm)

*If your fabric has a one-way print, be sure the pattern pieces are aligned in the same direction.

Fusible interfacing (for the facing): W 35⅜ in x L 27⅝ in
(90 cm x 70 cm)

Stay tape (for the front neckline): W ⅝ in x L 31½ in
(1.5 cm x 80 cm)

Elastic (for the cuffs): 8 cord x L 18⅞, 19⅝, 21¼, or 22¹⁄₁₆ in
(48, 50, 54, or 56 cm) (including the seam allowance)

Hooks and eyes x 6 (small)

Instructions

Preparation: Attach the fusible interfacing to the facing. Attach the stay tape to the front neckline. Overlock or zigzag the seam allowance on the bodice shoulders, back sides, sleeve seams, and shoulders of the collar ruffle.

1 Join the shoulders of the collar ruffle (press open the seam allowance) and sew the edge with a threefold hem. Gather the edge that you will be attaching to the neckline and front bodice.

2 Sew the bust darts (turning the darts upward), and then overlock or zigzag the seam allowance on the front sides.

3 Sew the shoulders (press open the side seam allowance).

4 Sew the sides (press open the side seam allowance). Sew the shoulders of the facing (press open the seam allowance), and then overlock or zigzag the seam allowance on the innermost edge of the facing.

5 Sandwich the collar ruffle between the bodice and the facing, and edge-stitch.

6 Make a threefold hem (see p. 39) and stitch the ruffle in place, working from the right side.

7 Sew the sleeve seams, leaving an opening for the elastic to pass through (press open the seam allowance).

8 Sew the cuffs with a threefold hem. Pass the elastic through the cuff.

9 Attach the sleeves (overlock or zigzag the seam allowance on both pieces at the same time. Turn the seam allowance toward the sleeves) (see p. 53).

10 Attach the hooks and eyes.

Cutting layout

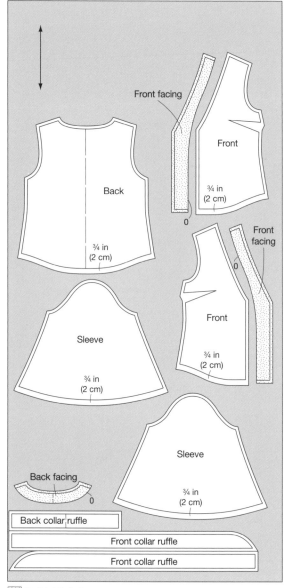

W 42½ in (108 cm)

Back
¾ in (2 cm)

Front facing

Front
¾ in (2 cm)

0

Front facing

Front
¾ in (2 cm)

0

Sleeve
¾ in (2 cm)

Sleeve
¾ in (2 cm)

Back facing
0

Back collar ruffle

Front collar ruffle

Front collar ruffle

Fusible interfacing

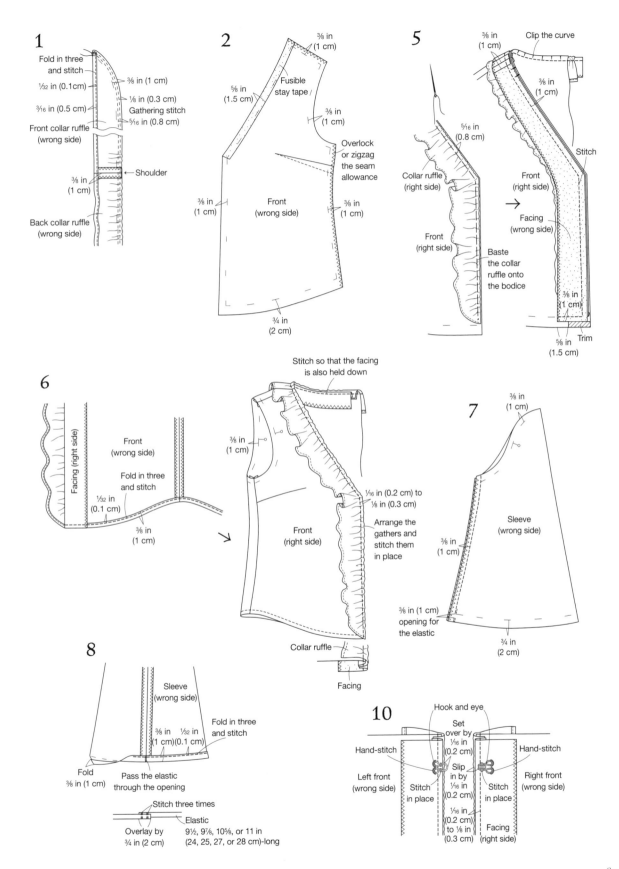

1

Fold in three and stitch
1/32 in (0.1 cm)
3/16 in (0.5 cm)
3/8 in (1 cm)
1/8 in (0.3 cm)
Gathering stitch
5/16 in (0.8 cm)
Front collar ruffle (wrong side)
3/8 in (1 cm)
← Shoulder
Back collar ruffle (wrong side)

2

3/8 in (1 cm)
5/8 in (1.5 cm)
Fusible stay tape
3/8 in (1 cm)
Overlock or zigzag the seam allowance
3/8 in (1 cm)
Front (wrong side)
3/8 in (1 cm)
3/4 in (2 cm)

5

3/8 in (1 cm)
Clip the curve
3/8 in (1 cm)
5/16 in (0.8 cm)
Collar ruffle (right side)
Stitch
Front (right side)
Front (right side)
Facing (wrong side)
Baste the collar ruffle onto the bodice
3/8 in (1 cm)
5/8 in (1.5 cm)
Trim

6

Facing (right side)
Front (wrong side)
Fold in three and stitch
1/32 in (0.1 cm)
3/8 in (1 cm)

Stitch so that the facing is also held down
3/8 in (1 cm)
Front (right side)
1/16 in (0.2 cm) to 1/8 in (0.3 cm)
Arrange the gathers and stitch them in place
Collar ruffle
Facing

7

3/8 in (1 cm)
Sleeve (wrong side)
3/8 in (1 cm)
3/8 in (1 cm) opening for the elastic
3/4 in (2 cm)

8

Sleeve (wrong side)
3/8 in (1 cm) 1/32 in (0.1 cm)
Fold in three and stitch
Fold
3/8 in (1 cm)
Pass the elastic through the opening
Stitch three times
Elastic
Overlay by 3/4 in (2 cm)
9½, 9⅞, 10⅝, or 11 in (24, 25, 27, or 28 cm)-long

10

Hook and eye
Set over by 1/16 in (0.2 cm)
Hand-stitch
Hand-stitch
Left front (wrong side)
Slip in by 1/16 in (0.2 cm)
Right front (wrong side)
Stitch in place
Stitch in place
1/16 in (0.2 cm)
1/16 in (0.2 cm) to 1/8 in (0.3 cm)
Facing (right side)

pattern VI
with darts

A-line dress

Fabric

Fabric [cotton Liberty print]: W 43¼ in x L 118⅛ in (110 cm x 300 cm)

*If your fabric has a one-way print, be sure the pattern pieces are aligned in the same direction.

Stay tape (for the zipper opening): W ⅝ in x L 39⅜ in (1.5 cm x 100 cm)

Invisible zipper: 20½ in (52 cm)

Fusible interfacing: 3⅛ in x 3⅛ in (8 cm x 8 cm)

Hook and eye x 1

Instructions

Preparation: Attach the fusible stay tape to the seam allowance of the zipper opening. Attach the fusible interfacing to the inner corner of the front and back skirts (see illustration 3). Attach the fusible interfacing to the L-shaped part of the front and back bodices.

Overlock or zigzag the seam allowance on the shoulders of the bodices, the center back, and the sleeve seams.

1 Sew the center back as far as the end of the opening (press open the seam allowance). Attach the invisible zipper (see p. 68).

2 Sew the bust darts (turning them upward).

3 Sew together the front and back skirts and side skirt panels (overlock or zigzag the seam allowance on both pieces at the same time. Turn the seam allowance toward the bodice and overlock or zigzag the seam allowance on the sides).

4 Sew the sides (press open the side seam allowance).

5 Make a threefold hem (see p. 39).

6 Sew the shoulders (press open the side seam allowance).

7 Pipe the neckline with the bias binding (using the same fabric as for the bodice) (see pp. 40–41).

8 Sew the sleeve seams (press open the seam allowance).

9 Gather the cuffs and pipe them with the bias binding (using the same fabric as for the bodice) (see pp. 40–41).

10 Attach the sleeves (overlock or zigzag the seam allowance on both pieces at the same time. Turn the seam allowance toward the sleeves) (see p. 53).

11 Attach the hook and eye at back neck.

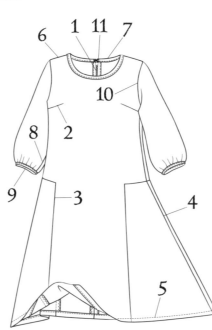

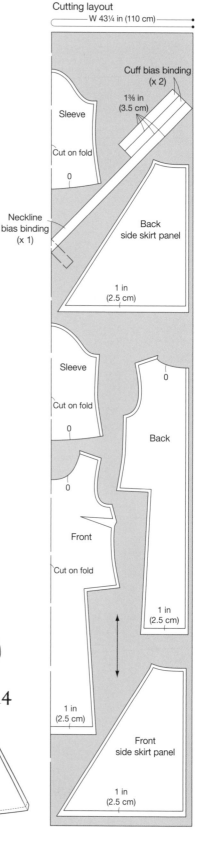

Cutting layout

W 43¼ in (110 cm)

Cuff bias binding (x 2)
1⅜ in (3.5 cm)

Sleeve
Cut on fold
0

Neckline bias binding (x 1)

Back side skirt panel
1 in (2.5 cm)

Sleeve
Cut on fold
0

Back
0

Front
Cut on fold
0

1 in (2.5 cm)

1 in (2.5 cm)

Front side skirt panel
1 in (2.5 cm)

3

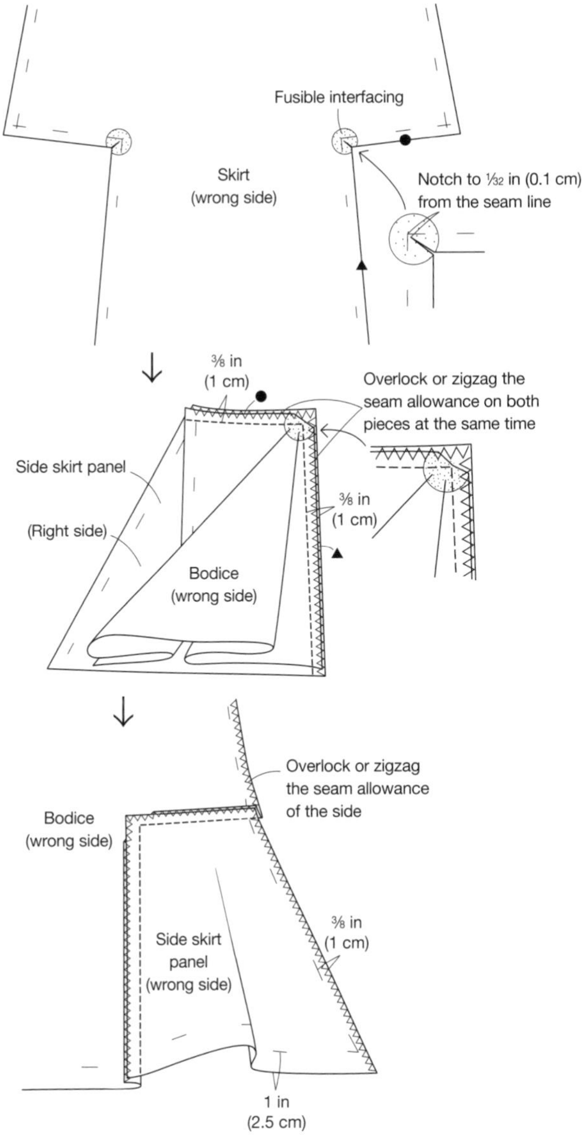

Fusible interfacing
Skirt
(wrong side)
Notch to 1/32 in (0.1 cm)
from the seam line
⅜ in
(1 cm)
Overlock or zigzag the
seam allowance on both
pieces at the same time
Side skirt panel
(Right side)
⅜ in
(1 cm)
Bodice
(wrong side)
Overlock or zigzag
the seam allowance
of the side
Bodice
(wrong side)
Side skirt
panel
(wrong side)
⅜ in
(1 cm)
1 in
(2.5 cm)

4

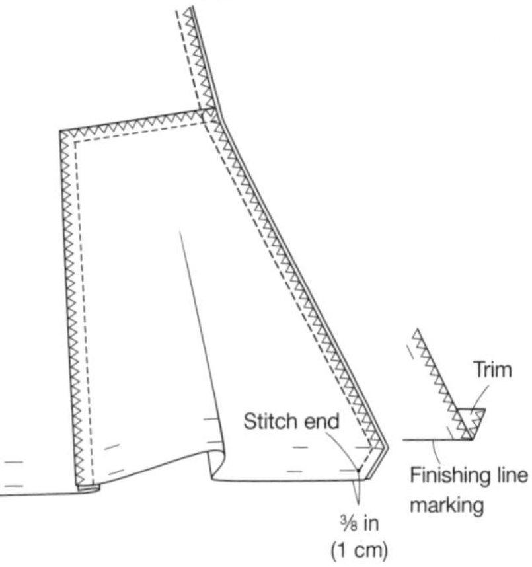

Trim
Stitch end
Finishing line
marking
⅜ in
(1 cm)

5

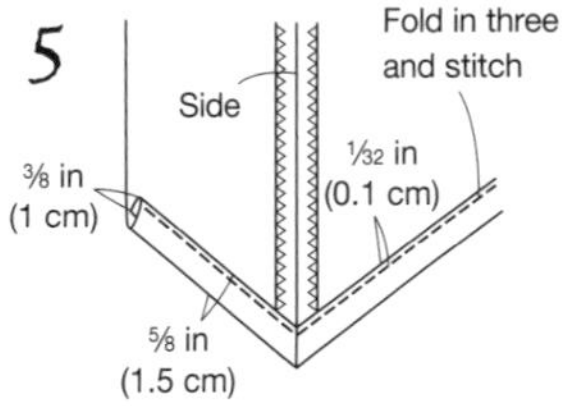

Fold in three
and stitch
Side
⅜ in
(1 cm)
1/32 in
(0.1 cm)
⅝ in
(1.5 cm)

7

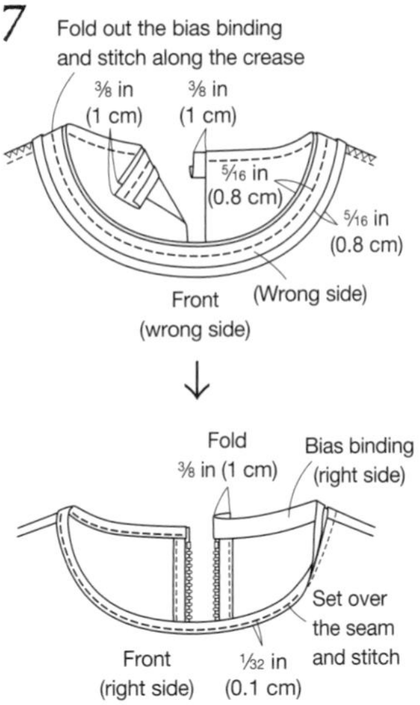

Fold out the bias binding
and stitch along the crease
⅜ in
(1 cm)
⅜ in
(1 cm)
5/16 in
(0.8 cm)
5/16 in
(0.8 cm)
Front
(wrong side)
(Wrong side)
Fold
⅜ in (1 cm)
Bias binding
(right side)
Set over
the seam
and stitch
Front
(right side)
1/32 in
(0.1 cm)

8

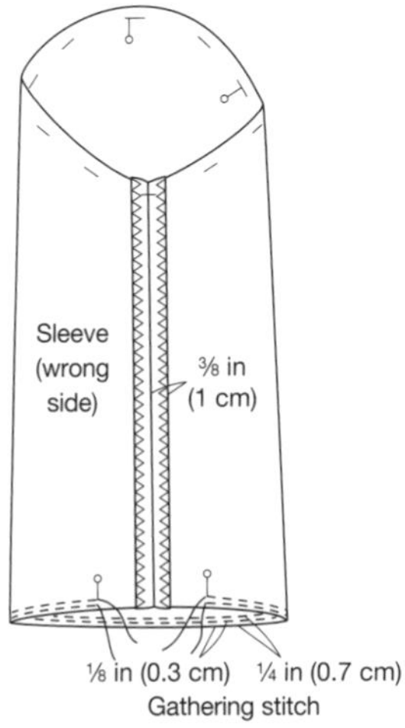

Sleeve
(wrong
side)
⅜ in
(1 cm)
⅛ in (0.3 cm)
¼ in (0.7 cm)
Gathering stitch

9

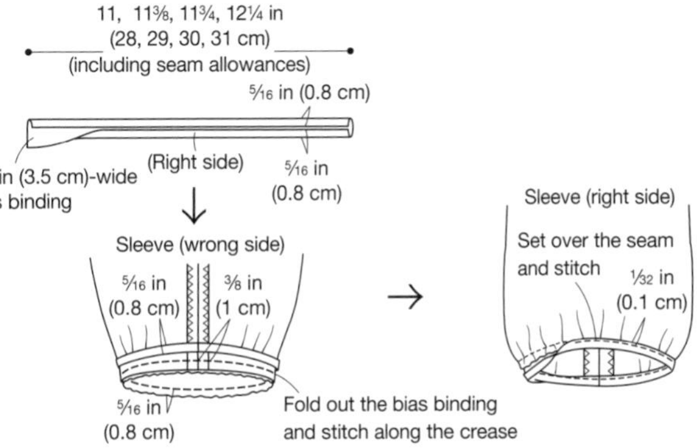

11, 11⅜, 11¾, 12¼ in
(28, 29, 30, 31 cm)
(including seam allowances)
5/16 in (0.8 cm)
1⅜ in (3.5 cm)-wide
bias binding
(Right side)
5/16 in
(0.8 cm)
Sleeve (wrong side)
5/16 in
(0.8 cm)
⅜ in
(1 cm)
5/16 in
(0.8 cm)
Fold out the bias binding
and stitch along the crease
Sleeve (right side)
Set over the seam
and stitch
1/32 in
(0.1 cm)

pattern VI
with darts

bell-sleeve coat dress

Fabric

Fabric [cotton and linen print]: W 43¼ in x L 102⅜ in (110 cm x 260 cm)
Fusible interfacing (for the facing): W 35⅜ in x L 43¼ in (90 cm x 110 cm)
Stay tape (for the front neckline): W ⅝ in x L 31½ in (1.5 cm x 80 cm)
Buttons: ⅝ in (1.8 cm) diameter x 6

Instructions

Preparation: Attach the fusible interfacing to the facing. Attach the stay tape to the front neckline. Overlock or zigzag the seam allowance on the bodice shoulders, back sides, and around the pocket.

1 Attach the pocket to the left front bodice.
2 Sew the bust darts (turning the darts upward), and then overlock or zigzag the seam allowances on the front sides.
3 Sew the shoulders (press open the seam allowance).
4 Sew the sides (press open the seam allowances).
5 Sew the shoulders of the facing (press open the seam allowance), and then overlock or zigzag the seam allowance on the innermost edge of the facing. Align the bodice and facing wrong sides out and edge-stitch.
6 Make a threefold hem (see p. 39).
7 Gather the sleeve seam ruffles and attach them to the sleeves (overlock or zigzag the seam allowance on both pieces at the same time. Turn the seam allowance toward the sleeves). Overlock or zigzag the seam allowance of the sleeve seams.
8 Sew the sleeve seams (press open the seam allowance).
9 Sew the cuffs with a threefold hem.
10 Attach the sleeves (overlock or zigzag the seam allowance on both pieces at the same time. Turn the seam allowance toward the sleeves) (see p. 53).
11 Make the buttonholes and attach the buttons.

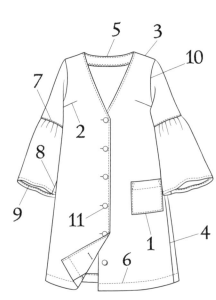

Cutting layout

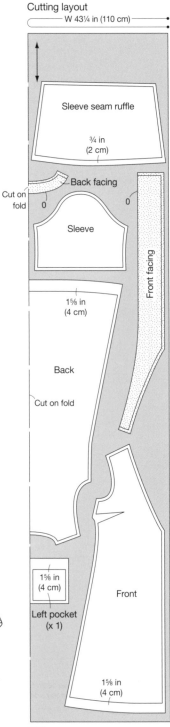

W 43¼ in (110 cm)

Sleeve seam ruffle
¾ in (2 cm)

Back facing

Cut on fold   0   0

Sleeve

Front facing

1⅝ in (4 cm)

Back

Cut on fold

1⅝ in (4 cm)

Left pocket (x 1)

Front

1⅝ in (4 cm)

Fusible interfacing

1

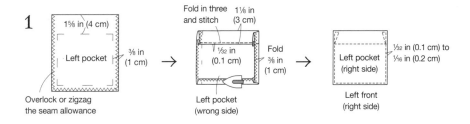

1⅝ in (4 cm)

Left pocket

⅜ in (1 cm)

Overlock or zigzag the seam allowance

Fold in three and stitch

1⅛ in (3 cm)

1/32 in (0.1 cm)

Left pocket (wrong side)

Fold ⅜ in (1 cm)

Left pocket (right side)

1/32 in (0.1 cm) to 1/16 in (0.2 cm)

Left front (right side)

5

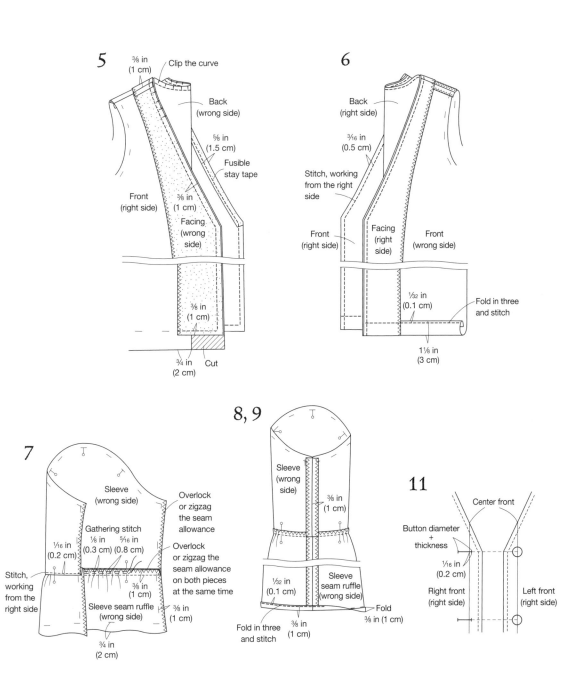

⅜ in (1 cm)

Clip the curve

Back (wrong side)

⅝ in (1.5 cm)

Fusible stay tape

Front (right side)

⅜ in (1 cm)

Facing (wrong side)

⅜ in (1 cm)

¾ in (2 cm)

Cut

6

Back (right side)

3/16 in (0.5 cm)

Stitch, working from the right side

Front (right side)

Facing (right side)

Front (wrong side)

1/32 in (0.1 cm)

Fold in three and stitch

1⅛ in (3 cm)

7

Sleeve (wrong side)

Gathering stitch

⅛ in (0.3 cm)

5/16 in (0.8 cm)

1/16 in (0.2 cm)

Stitch, working from the right side

Overlock or zigzag the seam allowance

Overlock or zigzag the seam allowance on both pieces at the same time

⅜ in (1 cm)

Sleeve seam ruffle (wrong side)

⅜ in (1 cm)

¾ in (2 cm)

8, 9

Sleeve (wrong side)

⅜ in (1 cm)

1/32 in (0.1 cm)

Sleeve seam ruffle (wrong side)

Fold ⅜ in (1 cm)

Fold in three and stitch

⅜ in (1 cm)

11

Center front

Button diameter + thickness

1/16 in (0.2 cm)

Right front (right side)

Left front (right side)

LAURENCE KING

Published in 2013 by Laurence King Publishing Ltd
361-373 City Road
London EC1V 1LR
United Kingdom
Tel: +44 20 7841 6900
Fax: +44 20 7841 6910
email: enquiries@laurenceking.com
www.laurenceking.com

Reprinted 2014

OTONA NO COUTURE SWEET DRESS BOOK PATTERN ARRANGE DE 23
STYLE NO DRESS BOOK
by Yoshiko Tsukiori
Copyright © Yoshiko Tsukiori 2011
All rights reserved.
Original Japanese edition published by EDUCATIONAL FOUNDATION
BUNKA GAKUEN BUNKA PUBLISHING BUREAU.

This English edition is published by arrangement with EDUCATIONAL
FOUNDATION BUNKA GAKUEN BUNKA PUBLISHING BUREAU, Tokyo
in care of Tuttle-Mori Agency, Inc., Tokyo

A catalogue record for this book is available from the British Library.

ISBN: 978-1-78067-108-6

Printed in China

Yoshiko Tsukiori
A graduate of Joshi Junior College of Art and Design,
Yoshiko Tsukiori worked for a variety of clothing
companies before establishing herself as an independent
sewing designer. Her expertise ranges from babywear and
children's clothing to womenswear.

Credits

Original Japanese edition

Cover design & layout: Mihoko Amano
Photography: Machiko Oodan (cover, pp. 1–36)
    Yasuo Nagumo (pp. 38–55)
Styling: Naoko Horie
Hair & makeup: Yumi Narai
Model: Mary
Cooking: THUMB AND CAKES
Tracing: Satomi Dairaku day studio
Sewing instructions: Mutsuko Sukegawa
Pattern grading: Akiko Kobayashi
Pattern tracing: Act A2
Proofreading: Masako Mukai
Editors: Tomoe Horie
    Norie Hirai (BUNKA PUBLISHING BUREAU)
Publisher: Sunao Onuma

English edition

Translated from the Japanese by Andy Walker
Technical consultants: Kevin Almond, Bo Breda, Chika Ito
Design and typesetting: Mark Holt
Commissioning editor: Helen Rochester (Laurence King Publishing)